Hanging-Bowls, Penannular Brooches and the Anglo-Saxon Connexion

David Longley

British Archaeological Reports 22
1975

British Archaeological Reports
122 Banbury Road, Oxford OX2 7BP, England

GENERAL EDITORS

A.C.C. Brodribb, M.A.
Mrs. Y.M. Hands

A.R. Hands, B.Sc., M.A., D.Phil.
D.R. Walker, B.A.

ADVISORY EDITORS

C.B. Burgess, M.A.　　　　　Neil Cossons, M.A., F.S.A., F.M.A.
Professor B.W. Cunliffe, M.A., Ph.D., F.S.A.
Sonia Chadwick Hawkes, B.A., M.A., F.S.A.
Professor G.D.B. Jones, M.A., D.Phil., F.S.A.
Frances Lynch, M.A., F.S.A.　　P.A. Mellars, M.A., Ph.D.
P.A. Rahtz, M.A., F.S.A.

B.A.R. 22, 1975: "Hanging-Bowls, Penannular Brooches and the Anglo-Saxon Connexion" © D.M.T. Longley, 1975.

The author's moral rights under the 1988 UK Copyright, Designs and Patents Act are hereby expressly asserted.

All rights reserved. No part of this work may be copied, reproduced, stored, sold, distributed, scanned, saved in any form of digital format or transmitted in any form digitally, without the written permission of the Publisher.

ISBN 9780904531251 paperback
ISBN 9781407318554 e-book
DOI https://doi.org/10.30861/9780904531251
A catalogue record for this book is available from the British Library
This book is available at www.barpublishing.com

CONTENTS

	Page
Acknowledgements	
List of Figures	
Introduction	1
Penannular Brooches	5
Hanging Bowls	15
Conclusions	32
Appendix (hanging-bowl groups)	37
Abbreviations	43
Bibliography	44

ACKNOWLEDGEMENTS

I would like to express my gratitude to Dr. Lloyd R. Laing of Liverpool University for his help and encouragement in the preparation of this paper, and to Mrs. S. C. Hawkes of Oxford University for her helpful comments.

LIST OF FIGURES

		Page
Fig. 1	Map: Romano-Saxon Pottery (data: Myres 1956 and 1959).	2
Fig. 2	Map: Early Germanic Pottery (data: Myres 1969).	2
Fig. 3	Map: Late Roman Military Metalwork (data: Hawkes and Dunning, 1961; Hawkes, 1974).	4
Fig. 4	Penannular brooch types (Fowler) F2, G, H2, H3 and H (Schematized and not to scale). Hanging bowl with Group 4a escutcheons. (Based on Loveden Hill, No. 1. Approx. ½ scale).	6
Fig. 5	a. Base of Cruciform brooch, Lyminge; b. Penannular brooch, Caerwent; c. Ox-head, Mountsorrel; d. Terminal of Caerwent brooch, 2/1; e. Ox-head, Ham Hill; f. Brooch, Alfriston, 2/1. (4b, c, d, e and f from photographs).	7
Fig. 6	Map: Penannular brooches, Types F, F1 and F2 (data: Fowler 1963 and Kilbride-Jones 1935-7).	9
Fig. 7	Map: Penannular brooches, Type G (data: Fowler 1963 with additions).	9
Fig. 8	Map: Penannular brooches, Types H, H1 and H/F (data: Fowler 1963 with additions).	11
Fig. 9	Map: Penannular brooches, Types H2 and H3 (data: Fowler 1963 with additions).	11
Fig. 10	Group 1 Hanging-bowl escutcheons: a, Hildersham: b, Castle Tioram: c, Baginton: d, Wilton: e, Tummel Bridge: f, Eastry: g, Faversham. (9b, d, e and g after Kilbride-Jones 1936-7; 9a, c and f from photographs).	17
Fig. 11	Map: Group 1 Hanging-bowl escutcheons and discs.	18
Fig. 12	Map: Group 2 Hanging-bowl escutcheons and discs.	18
Fig. 13	Group 2 Hanging-bowl escutcheons and discs: a, Dover No. 1; b, Baginton; c, Faversham; d, Winchester; e, Dover No. 3; f, Dover No. 2; g, Whitby.	21
Fig. 14	Group 3 Hanging-bowl discs: a, Camerton; b, Faversham; c, Kingston. Late Roman metalwork: d, Vermand; e, Coleraine hoard;	23

		Page
	f, Lydney; g, Colchester. Group 4b Hanging-bowl discs: h, Benty Grange; i, Faversham; j, disc found with Lullingstone bowl. (13b, c, h and i after Kendrick 1932; 13e after B.M. guide to Romano-British antiquities; 13g after Hawkes and Dunning, 1961; 13a, d and f from photographs; 13j after Henry 1936).	
Fig. 15	Group 4 Hanging-bowl escutcheons and discs; a, Hitchen; b, Chesterton on Fossway; c, Lullingstone; d, Barrington; e, Oving; f, Camerton No. 2; g, Stoke Golding, No. 1; h, Kingston No. 2; i, Stoke Golding, No. 2. (All after Kilbride-Jones 1936-7).	24
Fig. 16	Map: Group 3 Hanging-bowl escutcheons and discs.	26
Fig. 17	Map: Group 5 Hanging-bowl escutcheons.	26
Fig. 18	Group 5 Hanging-bowl escutcheons: a, Hawnby; b, Chessel Down; c, Finningley; d, Barton (no scale); e, Naunheim (no scale); f, Faversham; g, Sleaford; h, Benniworth; i, Hoprekstad; j, Whitby; k, Ballinderry. (17h after Kilbride-Jones 1963-7; 17k after Raftery 1966; 17a, b, c, d, e, f, g, i and j from photographs).	28
Fig. 19	Hanging-bowl rim forms. Late Roman: a, Naunheim; b, Straze bei Piest'any. Inbent: c, Chessel Down. Hammered: d, Baginton; f, Castle Tioram; g, Tummel Bridge. Fold over: 1, Winchester; i, Hawnby. Irish bowls: e, Ballinderry; j, Miklesbostad. (scale approx. $\frac{1}{2}$) Diagram to show the relative numbers of inbent, hammered and fold-over rims in each group. (19, a and b after Vierck; 19, c, d, f, g, h, i after Kilbride-Jones; 19 e and j after Henry).	31

All scales 1/1 except where indicated. Figs. 13 h and 17 i restored.

INTRODUCTION

The traditional image of an Anglo Saxon invasion, accompanied by fire and sword and with the native British being either massacred or driven westward, is no longer generally accepted.[1] Peaceful settlement is, however, difficult to prove. The material culture of the Anglo-Saxons and Sub-Roman Britons is, in many respects, very similar and indisputably 'British' objects are rare.[2] The result has been an Anglo-Saxon attribution to the majority of finds from the English areas in post 'Adventus' contexts.

It is becoming increasingly apparent that certain aspects of Germanic influence were being felt by the inhabitants of Eastern Britain to a not inconsiderable degree at a relatively early date. It is in such a situation that a familiarity with Germanic culture could be acquired by the Romano-Britons and vice versa. This must surely have eased the transition from Roman Britain to Anglo-Saxon England.

There is some evidence that Germanic settlement had begun as early as the mid-fourth century. Barbarian auxiliaries were used increasingly in the late Roman period and in Britain Allectus is known to have made use of barbarian mercenaries, possibly Franks recruited by Carausius before him, while Alamannic allies of Constantius, still in Britain, played an important part in the elevation of Constantine in 306.[3] Any nucleus of Germans settled in Britain could conceivably act as a focus for 'friends and relations' on the Continent. Evidence of a more tangible nature may be looked for in the pottery and metalwork of the period. Romano-Saxon pottery was first identified as a class by Myres.[4] This pottery is decidedly Eastern in distribution (Fig. 1) and is wheel thrown in Romano-British fabrics. In origin it is certainly Roman and the beginnings of the series are too early to have been influenced by any fourth century disposition of troops. Nevertheless in the later Roman period there does seem to have been a fruitful cross-fertilization between Roman and Germanic ceramics. Myres argues that this is a two-way process, although he places the Romano-Saxon series firmly on the 'Romano-British side of the cultural divide'. Nevertheless it is significant that the Romano-British potters were amenable to Germanic influence, and the distribution of the pottery points to the areas where this was to be found.

Myres has isolated certain classes of Germanic pottery which he considers to be suggestive of early settlement. These include: (1) cremation urns which may indicate the beginnings of certain cremation cemeteries in the late fourth century; (2) inhumation accessory vessels which may also date to the late fourth century; (3) the simple variety of Stehende Bogen urn and (4) Jutish and related types of pottery. These last two groups Myres considers to date from the first half of the fifth century in eastern England (Fig. 2).[5] The map shows that the same areas that produced Romano-Saxon pottery are involved except that the distribution is now more extensive. If the dating is correct the Germanic hand-made tradition continued alongside the Romano-Saxon Series and,

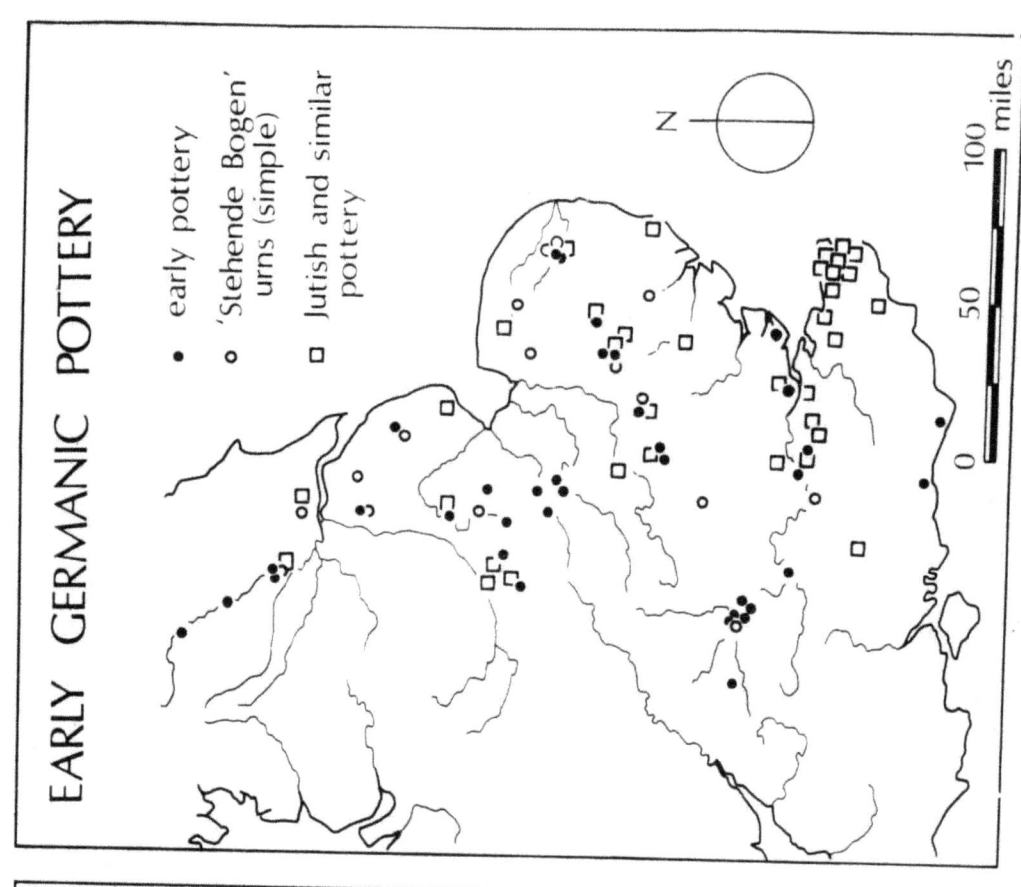

Fig. 2

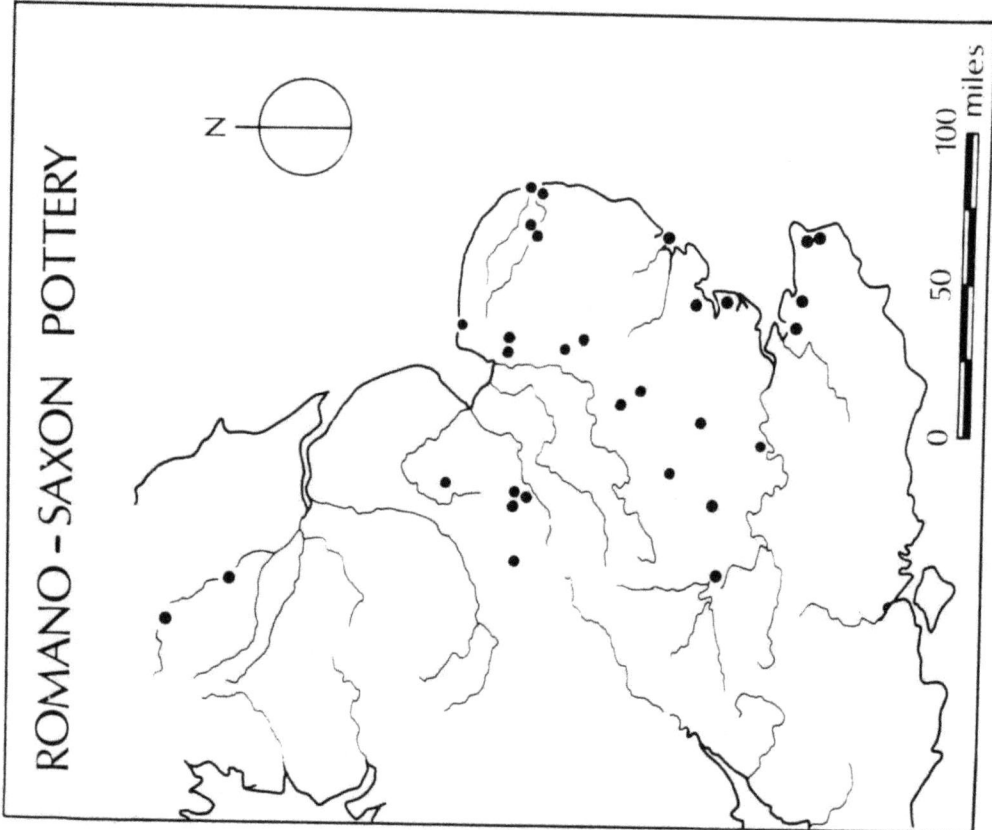

Fig. 1

with the breakdown of the Romano-British pottery industry in the late fourth-early fifth centuries, outlasted it. It is conceivable that 'Germanic' handmade pottery was in use by the native British after this had taken place, especially in consideration of Myres' views on the stylistic interchanges in the pottery of this period.[6]

In addition to the pottery, certain metalwork groups bear further study in this connexion. Late Roman belt fittings have been studied by Hawkes and Dunning and differentiated into various types.[7] These are essentially the fittings from military 'cingula' and in 1961 the question was posed 'does the whole series reflect some otherwise unknown disposition of troops?' Hawkes has pointed to Stevens' suggestion that barbarian 'Comitatenses' may have been billeted in the towns and on the rural estates of southern Britain[8] and she points out that these are the sort of belt fittings they would have used. Types IIIA, IV, VA, VI and VII have been assigned a continental manufacture and may, possibly, represent the belt fittings of the original 'Comitatus' if Stevens is followed.

Types I and II appear to have been made in British workshops and to have been introduced as a type around the same time, presumably developing from the original continental models. The evidence is by no means conclusive but it is possible that a significant proportion of the military users of these belt fittings were Germanic. Furthermore Mrs Hawkes hints that Type I buckles may, in fact, be an element of _female_ dress. (They are very narrow and all the Type I buckles from Saxon graves were worn by women). Belts were an element of Germanic female dress and 'with German elements present in the population from the middle of the fourth century it is not impossible that there were changes in the civilian dress of late Romano-British men and women.'[9]

Evison's theory of Frankish settlement south of the Thames in the early fifth century is not universally accepted.[10] Nevertheless it is not unreasonable to see, in the belt fittings decorated in the 'quoit brooch style', the emplacements of barbarian foederati, probably Germanic, in the first half of the fifth century.[11] If the demonstrable Germanic influence represents the existence of significant Germanic elements in the population of late Roman and Sub-Roman Britain then it becomes clearer why specifically sub-Romano-British styles seem to have left so little trace in the archaeological record. The early Anglo-Saxon metalwork may have become the logical outcome of the Romano-British metalworking tradition, increasingly Germanicized as settlement progressed. In many cases we must envisage peaceful cultural interchange with the newcomers living in close proximity to native British settlements in situations similar to those which may be inferred from the excavations at West Stow[12] and Chalton.[13]

Certain classes of object do occur in Anglo-Saxon contexts which are thought to be specifically Celtic, in either manufacture or inspiration. The objects in question are hanging-bowls and penannular brooches, and it is hoped that the discussion of these two selected groups may indicate an area where cross-cultural contact does seem to have taken place and that, furthermore, some aspects of Anglo-Saxon metalwork may be shown to owe their development to a continuation of the Romano-British tradition.

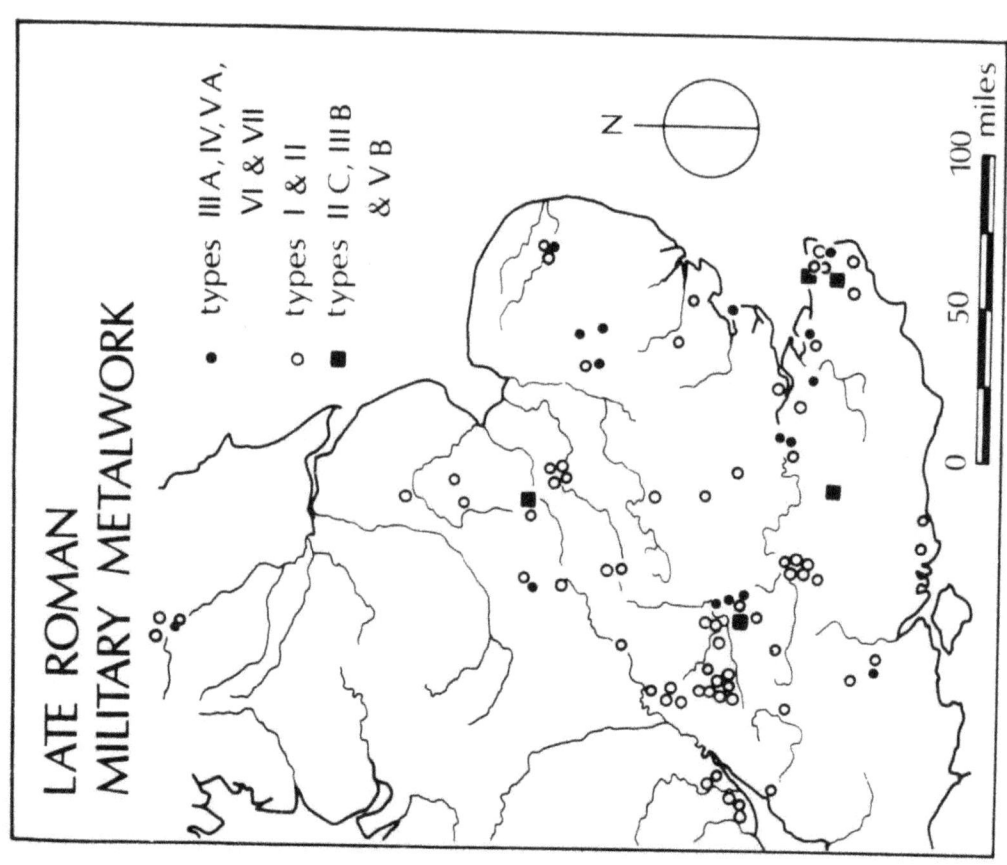

Fig. 3

PENANNULAR BROOCHES

The penannular brooch has been extensively studied, most recently by Elizabeth Fowler who has isolated the specifically Dark Age types as F, G and H but also includes A5, B3 and D7 as variants on older types.[14] In addition certain earlier types are frequently found in Anglo-Saxon graves, the context thereby dating them. These must represent survivals of brooch forms from the Romano-British period and, as Leeds noted, 'give the lie to the extermination of British inhabitants in the area of the settlements.'[15] Leeds suggested that on occasion, however, their occurrence in Anglo-Saxon graves might be due to looting from Roman villas, particularly where other specifically Roman finds were associated. On the other hand it is equally reasonable to see such examples as the result of trade or even as indicating the graves of sub-Romano-British natives. Leeds' main point, though, was that these penannulars were basically a British survival and gave rise to the more numerous classes of annular brooches in the English areas. In effect, therefore, the types of annular brooches commonly described as Anglo-Saxon are really the local development of the penannular brooch under the influence of Germanic metalwork styles, complementing the dissimilar development in the Highland Zone at this time. An interesting brooch in this development comes from Alfriston (Fig. 5f). It has a wide flattened hoop like a common annular type except that the hoop is not completed and it is, in fact, penannular. The pin, however, is fastened to an inner penannular, a device also met with on flattened annulars. The terminals of the Alfriston example are decorated with the heads of animals which remind one on the one hand of the opposed beast heads on late Roman military buckles, and, on the other, of the zoomorphic terminals of F brooches of southern Scotland and the Cotswolds. This brooch seems to be an intermediate stage between the true penannular and the wide annular types, possibly a development which took place in order to provide flat fields on the brooches which could accommodate the scroll work and 'quoit brooch animals' which were a common feature of metalwork in the south and east. This taste in metalwork is derived basically from the late Roman period, seen in Roman Britain in pieces similar to those of the Coleraine hoard and seen in Germanic contexts at Vermand (Fig. 14d and e).

This, then, is the postulated development of the penannular brooch in eastern England and the explanation for their widespread occurrence in 'Anglo-Saxon' graves. On the one hand, they represent survival of true Romano-British penannular types among the native British in this area (convincing support for this is demonstrated by the occurrence of the most common type of penannular in Anglo-Saxon contexts - type C - in the same area as its Romano-British distribution).[16] On the other hand they represent a development of the penannular type to provide a wider field in order to accommodate a certain late Roman taste in metalwork. There is no reason why this development should not have taken place spontaneously among the late Roman Britons although it is quite likely that Germanic influence in this part of England was a deciding element.

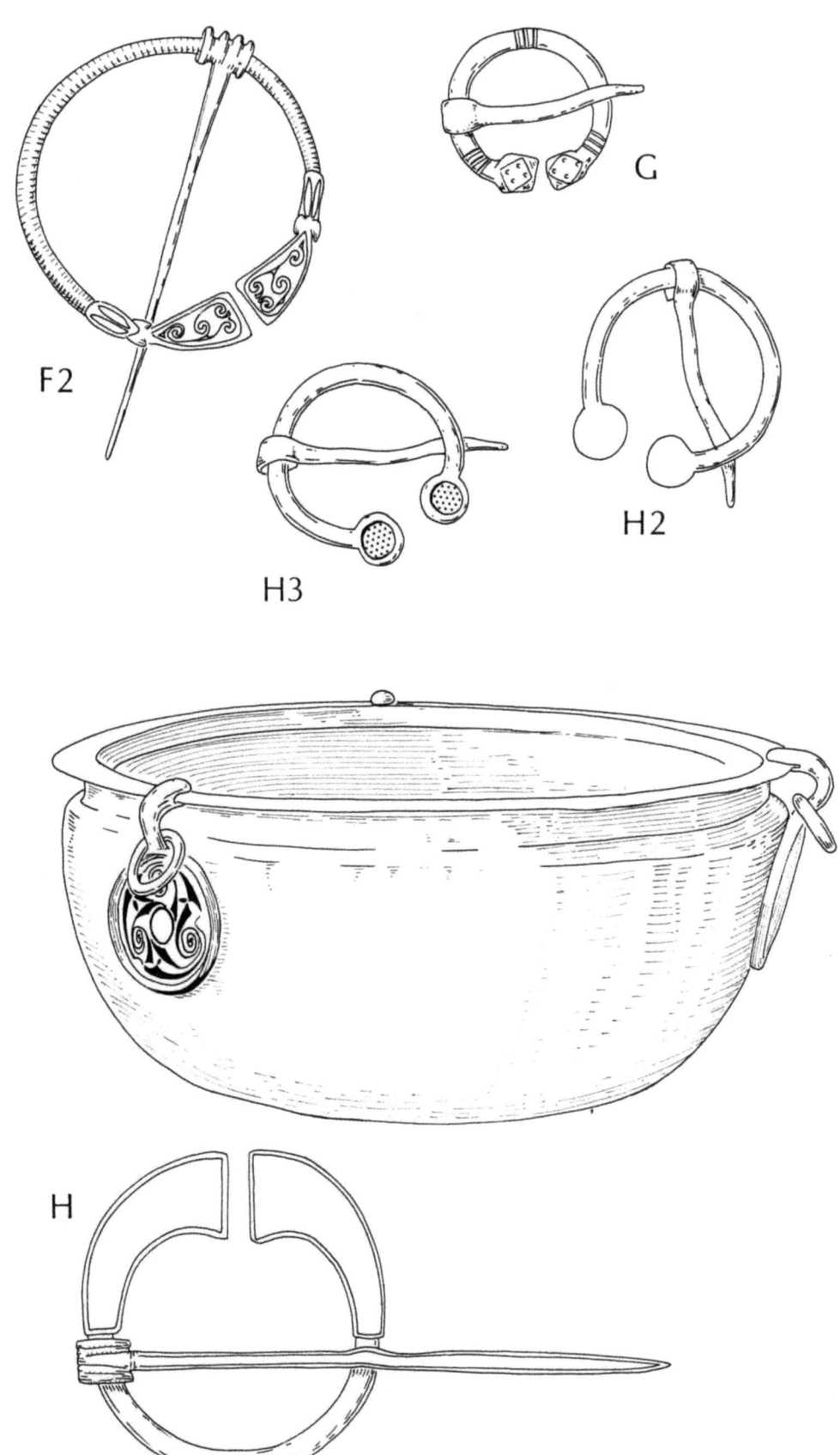

Fig. 4: penannular brooch types (schematized); hanging-bowl.

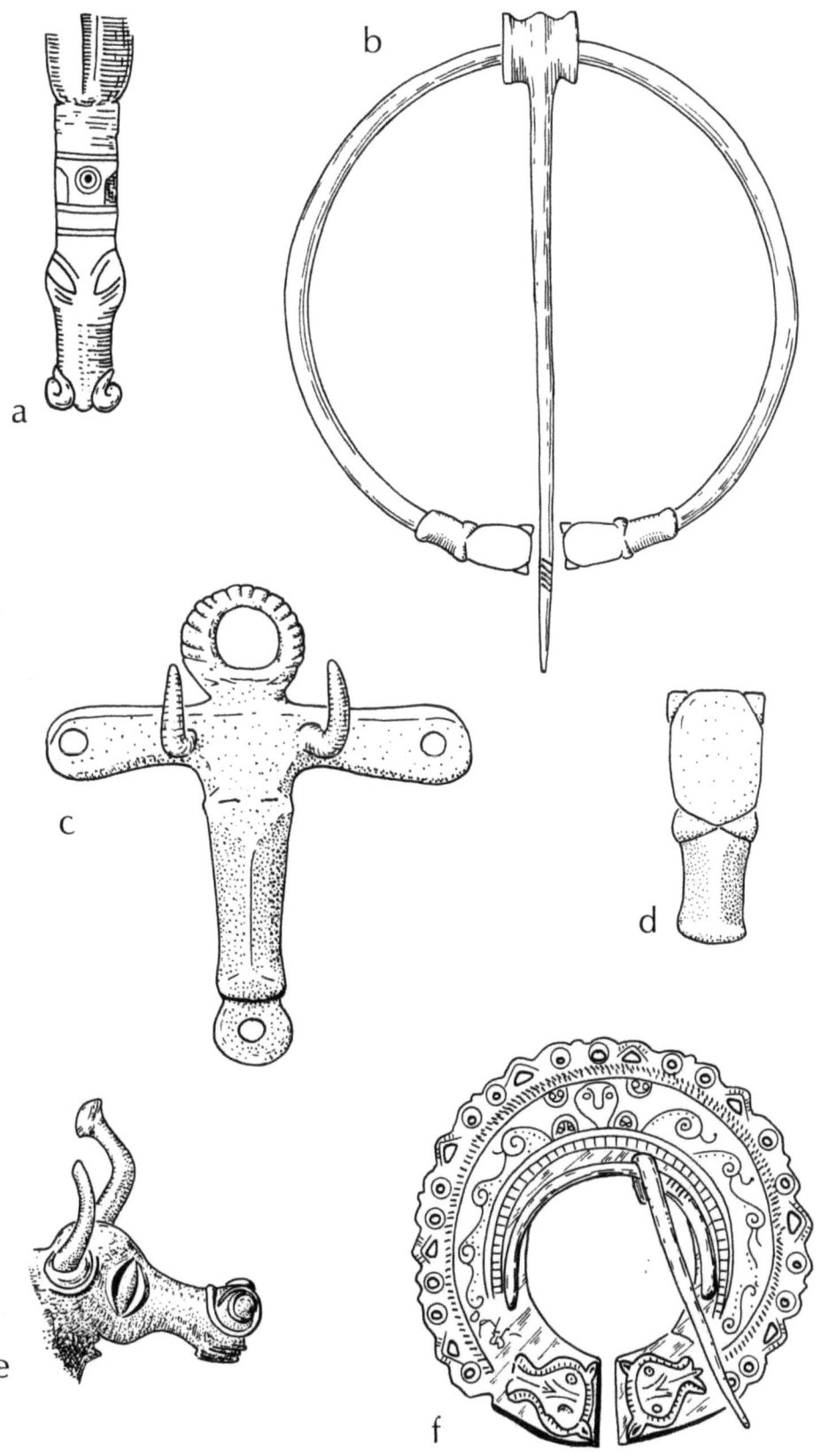

Fig. 5

In other parts of Britain the penannular brooch was developing along different lines. In the following discussion Elizabeth Fowler's classification is followed without, however, necessarily accepting her dating and its implications.

Type F

This is the familiar penannular brooch with 'zoomorphic' terminals. A good example is the Caerwent brooch (Fig. 5b). Fowler suggested that the prototype for F was the class E series which itself had developed out of the first century types D4 and D5.[17] No examples of E are reliably dated to any earlier than the fourth century, however, so it would seem that at some stage in the fourth century, at the earliest, type F developed out of the E class. The distribution of E is too generalised to indicate where this might have been except that Ireland can be ruled out. Fowler suggests Scotland due to the influence of first to third century Scottish snake bracelets while the fact that Roman snake armlets were reaching the Celtic west in the fourth century is demonstrated at Freestone Hill.[18] A first century spiral bracelet from Cambridgeshire points to similar influences in southern Britain, however, and it is significant that the Snailwell armlet belongs to the same south-western School as the Rose Ash bowl.[19]

It seems possible that type F could have originated in either Scotland or some more southerly region, probably during the fourth century. Two centres of production are indicated by the distribution map,(Fig. 6) one in southern Scotland and the other in the Severn/Avon region. The southerly distribution may have a significance which becomes more apparent in relation to the distribution of type G brooches so its discussion will be deferred for the moment. Type F was transmitted to Ireland, either from southern Scotland or the Bristol Channel, where elaboration with enamel (F1) and further elaboration with 'ultimate La Tene' decoration (F2) took place. This last feature was a peculiarly Irish development as regards the F series for although F2s were probably made on mainland Britain, as the lead die from Dinas Powys indicates, this is surely a result of Irish influence.[20] The two F brooches from Gwynedd are also best seen as the result of trade with Ireland although the migration of Cunedda and his band might provide an alternative context.

C. F. C. Hawkes has shown how it was possible for a native tradition of bronze working to persist through the Roman period, possibly to emerge again with the breakdown of Roman mass production.[21] In particular, Hawkes was concerned with ox-head bucket attachments and showed that this Celtic tradition survived best, though not unaffected by Roman realism, in Wales and the West Midlands. He did, however, detect a barbarisation creeping in at the end of the series that was neither Roman nor Celtic. The Twyford example must represent this as does possibly the 1956 escutcheon from Dinorben.[22] Now that doubt has been cast on the Anglian associations of the Twyford escutcheon both may possibly be dated late third century.[23] On the other hand there is more than a suspicion that something of the purer Celtic tradition survived the Roman occupation and this will be discussed below with reference to the cruciform brooch series. For the present purpose the late third century ox-head from Mountsorrel is of great importance (Fig. 5c). This example is far from the curves and spirals of the Ham Hill and Dinorben 1912 escutcheons yet it is

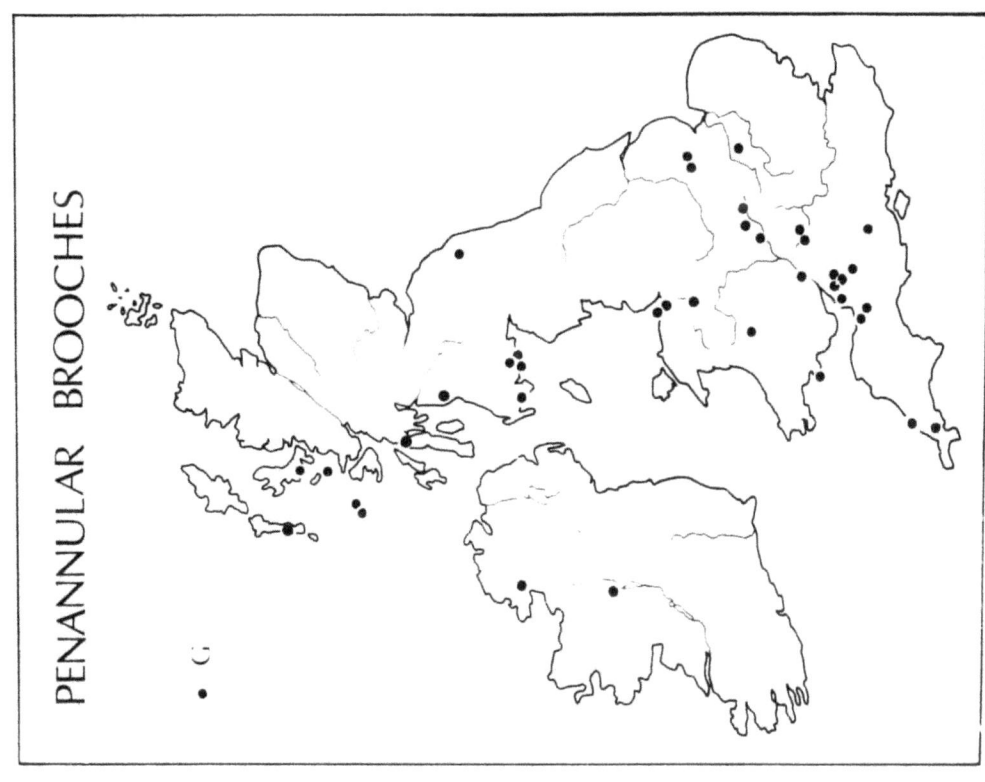

Fig. 7

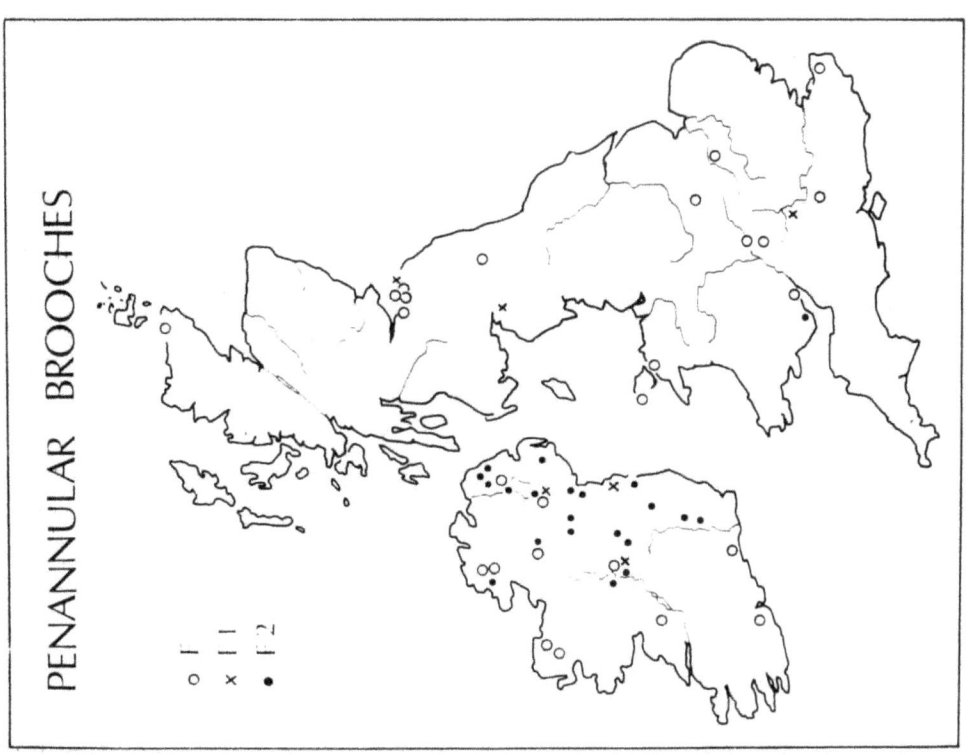

Fig. 6

equally far from Roman realism and in its stylization it must represent a continuation or, rather, a development of the Celtic tradition.[24] In the present context its importance lies in the similarity between this piece and the terminals of type F penannular brooches. The similarity is so striking that ox-heads such as the Mountsorrel example must represent one of the major influences behind the development of type F (Fig. 5c and d). An example of type F actually comes from the same area.[25] A curious feature in this development of the 'ox-head' - now minus horns - is that later examples of the F series, particularly those which occur in Ireland seem to get closer to the Iron Age originals in their curving and unpraised snouts.[26] A particularly striking example comes neither from the Celtic area nor from a penannular brooch - the animal head at the base of a cruciform brooch from Lyminge with its almond eyes and spiral nostrils is so much in the style of the Ham Hill escutcheon that one wonders what spans the five hundred years or so that divides them (Fig. 5a and e).

Type H

This type has a stronger claim to Scottish ancestry. It has flat expanding terminals well seen in the Pant-y-Saer brooch. Fowler derives type H from Aa penannulars, certain Scottish examples of which have significantly flattened terminals which seem to foreshadow H. One of the most interesting features of H brooches is their distribution (Fig. 8). The five occurrences in eastern England are all, as far as can be ascertained, in Anglo-Saxon contexts and this must date these particular examples to the late fourth century at the very earliest. The coin evidence for the Norrie's Law examples, if these are really brooches, has been discredited so these are no help in dating and the hanging-bowl escutcheon from Tummel Bridge is an old one, whereas the brooches are new, so the dating of this hoard must remain uncertain, even assuming there was agreement on the hanging-bowl.[27]

Three factors, however, may help to narrow down the limits of this series. (1) H brooches are absent from Traprain Law. This is suggestive that the series does not begin before the early fifth century. (2) The occurrence at Anglo-Saxon sites but absence from Romano-British sites argues for a date when Romano-British sites can no longer be distinguished as such - possibly 450 plus. (3) Moulds for a developed form of H, at the moment unique and possibly forming a bridge between the original type H and the more florid types which occur in Irish contexts such as the Tara brooch, occur at the Mote of Mark.[28] This site was occupied from the fifth century to the early seventh.[29]

All in all, then, it would appear that the main currency of type H took place between the early fifth century and the late sixth century. From an origin in Scotland type H was disseminated down the east coast one way and to Ireland the other. The east coast examples probably represent a dispersion of influence along this coast from Pictland to the Anglo-Saxon areas and when the hanging-bowl series is discussed it is hoped that this will be seen as a two-way process. In Ireland type H picks up enamel and becomes type H1. 'Trade' from Ireland will then account for the Kenfig and Scilly Isles examples of H1. The plain H brooch from Pant-y-Saer could also have come from Ireland (the long pin looks Irish). It may be a mistake to associate (as Fowler does) H brooch provenances with those of E ware especially with a view to using this to date the brooches.[30]

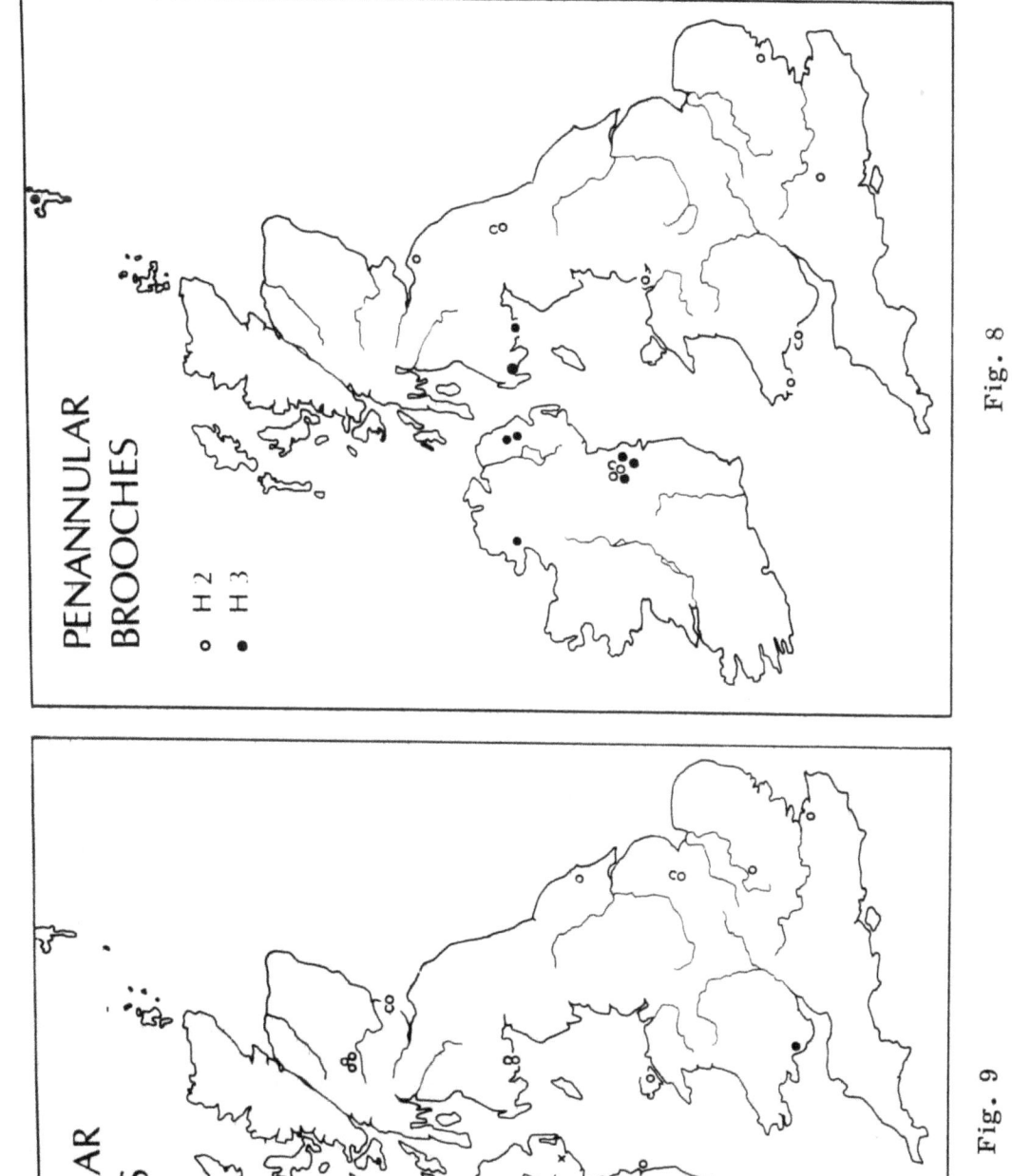

Fig. 8

Fig. 9

Nevertheless, a similar sort of west coast trade route does seem to be in operation although probably at a slightly earlier date. E ware is already known from Fife and Midlothian and perhaps more remains to be recognised along the east coast in Anglo-Saxon contexts.[31] If this is the case then, the H brooches (and hanging-bowls, see below) probably represent an earlier manifestation of seaborne contact down both the east and west coasts of Britain linking not only the Celtic areas but Picts and Anglo-Saxons as well. A and B ware also attest to trade connexions in the fifth and sixth centuries but only round the southern half of the Irish Sea.[32]

Type H/F

This composite type combines elements of both type H and type F. It occurs only in Ireland and possibly developed there with the arrival of H brooches out of the already present F types. Plain type H is relatively uncommon in Ireland, soon developing into the composite class which in turn leads on to the richer class of brooch exemplified by pieces such as the Tara and Breadalbane brooches.

Type H2

This type (see Fig. 9) has circular flattened terminals. Fowler has suggested a Romano-British origin for this type on the basis of its provenances.[33] The Silchester example could be later, however, as there is evidence for a continuation of occupation at Silchester into the fifth century and possibly later.[34] The Colchester example is somewhat anomalous but could have found its way down the east coast from Scotland. Nevertheless, the Traprain example, odd though it is, gives a T.A.Q. for the start of H2 in the late fourth century. It is also possible that the examples from Glamorgan, Pembroke and Cheshire are the result of Irish influence and in this respect the Ogam stone from Silchester is suggestive. The Silchester and Linney examples both have a similar decoration of incised lines on the terminals. If this is in fact the case H2 is seen as a southern Scottish or Irish development rather than Romano British, although late fourth century is an acceptable starting point for the series.

Type H3

This enamelled variant is basically an Irish elaboration and the series is confined mainly to Ireland. A further development of the circular terminal type, however, became very popular in Pictland. This is the type with a central boss surrounded by cast ribbing which later sprouted lateral projections or cusps.[35] A mould, in all probability for a brooch of the Croy type, was found in the 1913 Mote of Mark excavations.[36] The Mote of Mark, therefore, provides evidence for the continuation of the enamelled H3 series into the sixth century and also for the beginnings of the Pictish form at least by the late sixth century.[37]

Type D7

For this type with castellated terminals there is little that can be added to Fowler's suggestion that this is a post Roman elaboration on the widespread Romano-British D6 brooch. An origin in the south-east is envisaged (Colchester, Richborough and Woodcutts) while the type is carried west and elaborated in the post Roman period (Dunadd, Castletown and Cork).[38]

Type G

This is the most numerous Dark Age penannular brooch in mainland Britain. The type is characterized by thickened faceted terminals often decorated with four dots within a lozenge.[39] Fowler suggests that G developes out of D or E and that it possibly begins at the same time as F.[40] This would place its origin in the late 4th century and the roughly similar southerly distribution of the two types (Figs. 6 and 7) suggests that they are contemporary. There are significant differences however: (1) G is far more widespread in southern Britain; (2) G is virtually absent from Ireland; (3) G is absent from Traprain Law whereas there are three examples of F. This is important for it would seem to indicate that G had not come into fashion before the beginning of the fifth century.

The absence from Traprain might be due to local preference but there are G types in Southern Scotland and moulds from the Mote of Mark and Dunadd indicate that they were being made there in the fifth and sixth centuries. Nevertheless, perhaps a broad contemporaneity is indicated involving the same two metalworking areas - southern Scotland and the Severn/Cotswold area - as type F. A further indication that type G might be later than F is the boundary line G distribution seems to trace along the general direction of the Fosse Way. It is tempting to see this as a demarcation between possible Celtic and Saxon areas. Such a dichotomy is not likely to have been apparent in the late fourth century, despite the presence of Germanic federates in the Dorchester region: in fact it has been argued that there was a certain amount of mixing of cultures at this period. What seems to be represented in the type G distribution is a situation where a polarization may have been taking place, possibly from the late fifth century onwards, a feature not evident in type F distribution. A late fifth century date is at least suggested by the association of one of the Fairford brooches with two saucer brooches. The fact that some of these G brooches do occur in 'Anglo-Saxon' contexts may imply some sort of cultural interchange along the border. A starting point around the mid-fifth century, therefore, is suggested for the G series. The scarcity of the type in Ireland is possibly due to the fact that type F was already well established. The distribution map of type G again indicates widespread connexions along the west coast of Britain, a very late example occurring in the ninth century Trewhiddle hoard in Cornwall being parallelled by a brooch from Skye.[41]

CONCLUSIONS

From a study of the penannulars of this period certain trends emerge. In eastern England an evolution took place from the penannular to the wide flat annular under the influence of late Roman metalwork styles although much older penannular types continue, perhaps, to be produced for a market lower down the social scale. In the north and west new variations on the traditional penannular were produced. These show a considerable overlap in dating and regional distribution and on the one hand probably reflect the difference between expensive and cheap brooches and, on the other, a considerable amount of contact between the supposedly different areas of Dark Age Britain. Coastwise links down east and west Britain are evident as well as connexions between the west coast of Britain and Ireland. The distribution maps of various types of penannular brooches probably represent an extension of the trade along the western seaways already indicated by the distribution of Mediterranean and Gaulish imported pottery.[42]

Anglo-Saxon objects have been occasionally identified at Dark Age sites in the west. Rhineland glass, for example, occurs in considerable quantity at the Mote of Mark and Dinas Powys. It is unlikely that the fragments recovered represent the use of Germanic glassware by the Celts, who do not seem to have been able to manufacture their own, but rather that the broken glass was brought to the site for the manufacture of enamels. Germanic scrap metal also occurs at Dinas Powys and there is no reason why these raw materials should not have been obtained through trade.[43] Similarly a number of Celtic penannulars occur in Anglo-Saxon contexts and, although it has been suggested that these may represent plunder, H brooches in eastern England can hardly represent plunder from Pictland. Trade must here be envisaged and if here why not, for example, in the case of the F and G brooches of the west Midlands.

HANGING BOWLS

The hanging-bowl 'problem' has provoked much controversy and a divergence of opinion which has been confined not only to the dating of the objects but also to their use, origins and makers. Each study has resulted in a new solution, the latest, by Mrs. Fowler almost denying the existence of a problem at all.[44]

The 'problem' of the hanging-bowls lies in the fact that the great majority have been discovered in Anglo-Saxon contexts while at the same time displaying elements that are at once Celtic in 'feel' and foreign to the Anglo-Saxon repertoire. Using Fowler's catalogue as a starting point a new attempt has been made to define five main groups based on the shape and design of escutcheons and discs.

The appendix lists the discs and escutcheons from approximately 85 different bowls. The classification is, however, of individual discs or escutcheons and where dissimilar escutcheons occur on the same bowl these have been listed separately. A typology of hanging bowls can only be fully meaningful if the bowls are considered as a whole and size, rim forms etc. taken into account. On the other hand many of the escutcheons are not known in association with any bowl. The groupings therefore are of complete discs and escutcheons (not of decorative elements abstracted from their context on the escutcheon) and it is hoped that this method will prove useful in providing a general picture of the contemporaneity or otherwise, and more particularly, the distribution of certain fashions on hanging bowls.

The dating of these bowls has by no means been firmly established, partly through a lack of datable associations, if any, and partly through a lack of agreement on the stylistic influences involved. It is also quite possible that the bowls had a long life before they were buried or discarded and in some instances escutcheons have been found pierced, evidently for hanging as pendants.[45]

FUNCTION

The use of hanging bowls has recently been fully discussed in an important article by Dr. Vierck.[46] It is there suggested that the type evolved from Late Roman bowls with suspension rings which were commonly employed in conjunction with tripod stands. The folding tripod was a common Late Roman device for supporting bowls, however, and was not limited to a single function, so while it may be accepted that hanging bowls were, in fact, supported by tripods it is still by no means clear what function they fulfilled. It is conceivable that similar bowls could be put to divergent uses and among those possible are as baptismal bowls, handwashing at the table, ritual lustration and wine serving or mixing. Dr. Vierck seems to favour a religious context for the bowls, seeing in them a development from the ritual tripod of the classical period to a close connexion with the Christian Church from its inception in Britain.[47] While some of the bowls in all probability did find use in the Christian Church and some do seem to bear specifically Christian symbolism (e.g. Whitby No. 1), the present state of the evidence would seem to indicate a secular use for the majority of the bowls. The association of ladles with the escutcheons at Whitby and the bowls at Sutton Hoo, the close connexion of the drinking horn complex with the smaller bowls from Sutton Hoo and a palm cup and drinking horn mounts with one of the Loveden Hill bowls suggests that the bowls may have been receptacles for drink; possibly wine, as iron bound wooden beer or mead buckets also occur at Sutton Hoo and Loveden Hill.[48] The 'Gododdin' informs us that the Britons drank wine out of glass, gold and silver vessels and beer and mead out of drinking horns in the late sixth century and the 'Gwarchan Tudfwlch' describes the hero as 'trybedawt rawt' which is taken to mean that the host (the hero) has many tripods ('trybedawt') at his disposal with which to entertain his guests.[49] The hanging bowl was certainly a prestige item as its inclusion in many Anglo-Saxon graves testifies and it may be that this prestige was contained in the warrior's ability to entertain his guests.

The majority of bowls associated with burials come from inhumations while only 4 are known from cremations (all from Loveden Hill). In two cases at Loveden Hill hanging bowls actually contained the cremation. Cremations in metal bowls are also known from other sites and it has been suggested that this practice belongs to the later period of heathenism rather than to the earlier phases of settlement.[50] Hanging bowls in inhumations have also been known to contain food offerings as instanced by the onions and crab apples at Ford Down.[51] While so few bowls have been found with any dateable associations, most of those that have would seem to belong to the seventh century.

Group 1. (Figs. 10 and 11). This group includes all the openwork escutcheons and is subdivided to take into account differences in the openwork pattern. The Eastwell escutcheon is typical of group 1a. Eastwell itself is plain, as is Castle Tioram, although the Baginton and Hildersham escutcheons are decorated. 1b is an openwork design very similar to 1a although four peltas are involved in the make-up as opposed to the two of group 1a. The two escutcheons which at present comprise this group are not strictly identical. The Tunnel Bridge example does, however, appear to be a negative of the Wilton pattern. There does also seem to be a link between the two escutcheons of 1c in the ornamented horseshoe shape around a central element and the circular element at the base of the hoop. This is seen as a rosette on the Eastry example and as the curls in the animals' tails on Faversham No. 1.

The design of the 1a and 1b escutcheons is so similar that some connexion must be envisaged although the distribution map offers no solution (see Fig. 11). The Tummel Bridge bowl has been dated to the fifth century by association with type H penannulars in the same hoard, whereas another bowl with Group 1 escutcheons from Hildersham has been dated to the seventh century by its context in a warrior burial of that date. The Hildersham bowl has applied animals which may be compared with those of the Lullingstone bowl,

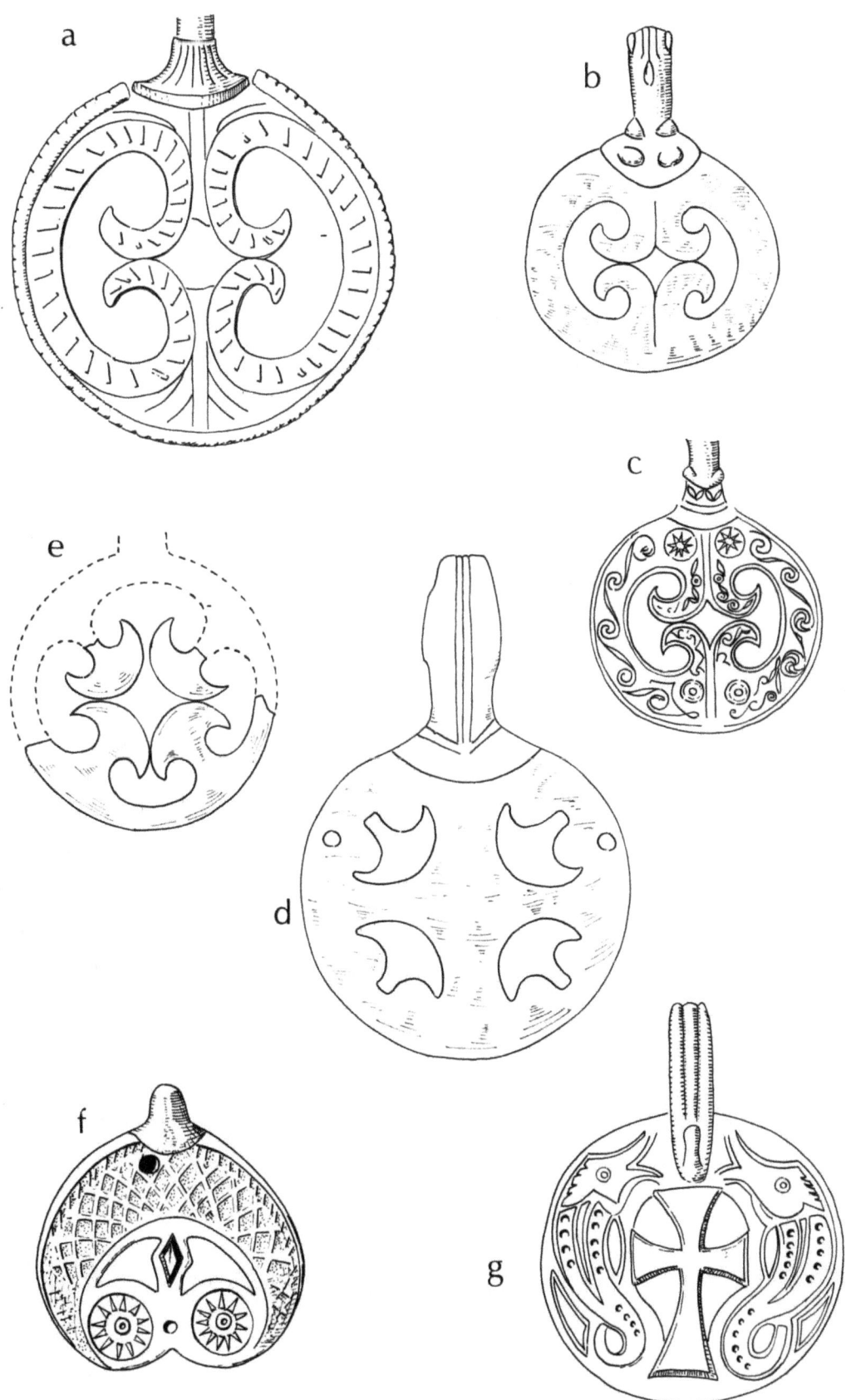

Fig. 10

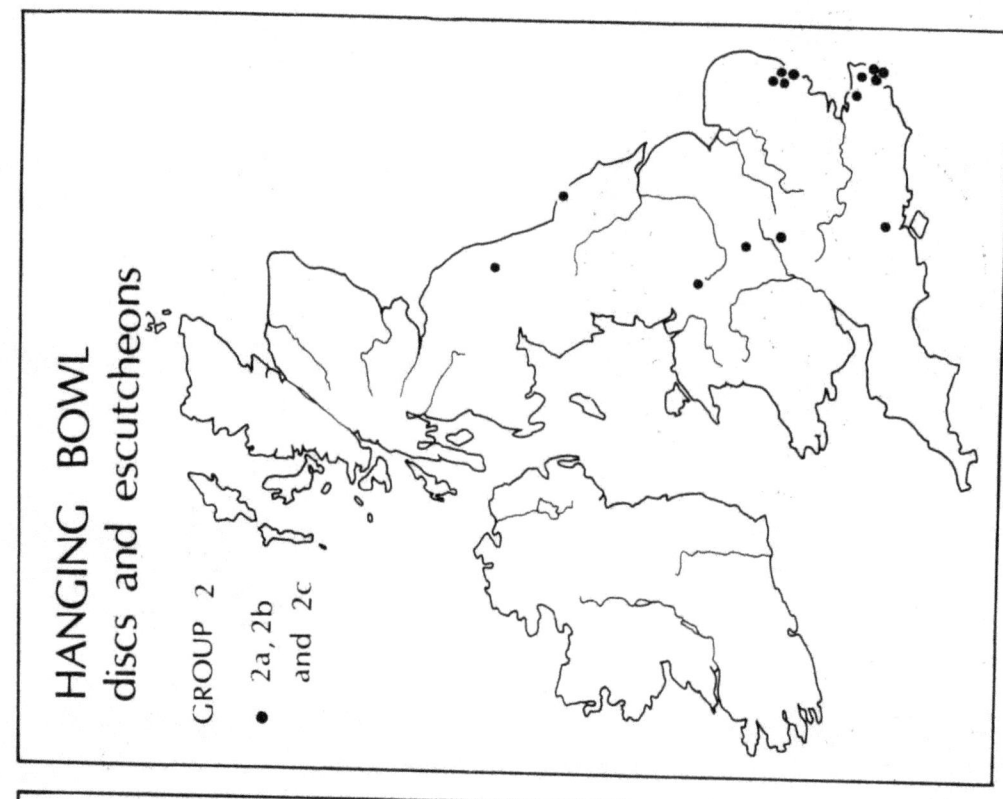

Fig. 12

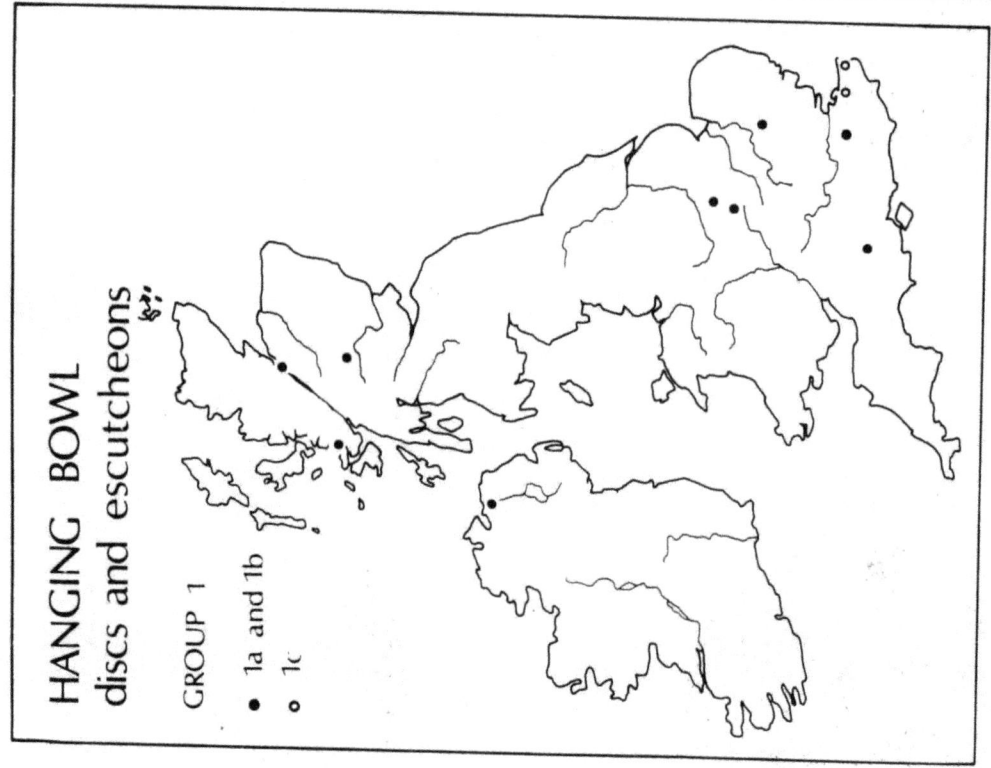

Fig. 11

for which a late sixth-early seventh century date will be suggested below, and applied bands which are similar to the sixth-seventh century 'belt mount' from Droxford, Hants.[52] It should be noted that the Hildersham bowl is in a very fragmentary condition and was probably old when buried. A date range from the fifth to the late sixth-early seventh centuries may, therefore, be suggested for this group. Not everyone would accept a fifth century date for the Tummel Bridge example but allowing a fifth/sixth century date for the deposition of the hoard on the evidence of the penannulars (see page   ) and, given the fact that the brooches are new, whereas the escutcheon is old, then a fifth century date for the escutcheon seems reasonable. Furthermore, the Tummel Bridge escutcheon provides a link between such Roman pieces as the Richborough and Jewry Wall openwork plaques.[53] A continuation of this motif over a considerable period, then, seems likely.

Group 1c consists of the openwork escutcheons from Eastry and Faversham (Fig. 10, f and g) Ozanne suggested that the Faversham escutcheon cannot date earlier than 640.[54] This assumption rests on three arguments: (1) the similarity between the Faversham animals and the Benty Grange animals which Haselhoff considered to be specifically Celtic; (2) Haselhoff's belief that Celtic influence on Anglo-Saxon ornament does not ante-date Irish missionary activity beginning c. 634;[55] (3) that the Faversham escutcheon is 'patently Christian'. The opposed animal motif is, however, very ancient and the same forms crop up again and again.[56] Often a central figure was included in the design, symbolizing the Great Goddess or Lord of the beasts and this religious symbolism was perpetuated in the Dark Ages by Christianizing the subject into 'Daniel in the Lion's Den'. In the case of the Faversham example, it has been argued, a cross fulfills this function. A Christian context need not be the case in the Faversham example; the motif certainly need not be due to Celtic influence - opposed beast are just as much a part of the Germanic heritage as the Celtic. Late Roman metalwork found, for example, in the graves of Germanic mercenaries on the Continent is relevant to the Faversham escutcheon and Vermand provides good examples (Fig. 14d). Amongst them a spear mount has two pairs of beasts very similar to the Faversham ones with punched dot decoration - the difference being that the Vermand ones are disposed back to back. The top pair even has a geometric ornament which could be interpreted as a cross between the animals. Of even greater relevance are the numerous buckles, attributed by Hawkes and Dunning to late fourth century military units in Britain.[57] A derivative 'British' type of possibly late fourth century date from Colchester (see Fig. 14g) has two opposed beasts which bear a striking resemblance to the Faversham beasts. They have punched dot decoration, large ring and dot eyes, the gaping 'snout' and the comb element. The pin is vaguely cruciform in shape and is even more so on other examples. It is difficult not to see some form of influence from one piece to the other. Strengthening the evidence in favour of seeing the influence of late Roman belt fittings behind group 1c are a group of buckles from the late fourth century Romano British temple at Lydney.[58] Two (nos. 130 and 101) belong to the same group as the Colchester example, but the third, described by Wheeler as a 'common Roman type' is very suggestive of the shape of the Faversham escutcheon (excepting the fact that the buckle is devoid of decoration) (Fig. 14f). This buckle must be late fourth century in date. Ignoring the reasonable possibility that the Faversham cross might be no more than a decorative element, a Christian symbol would nevertheless not be out of place in late fourth century early fifth century Kent. In consequence a date for 1c around 400 is suggested.

Group 2. The distinguishing feature of group 2 is the division of the escutcheon or disc into two elements; an ornamented border zone around a central element. In the majority of extant examples the border zone takes the form of a running scroll or a variation on this. Group 2a has an ornamented central element and an exterior scroll work panel. Although strictly, group 2a should comprise two independent zones in some examples the central element becomes assimilated with the border zone, probably under the influence of the group 4 design. This can be seen on the Faversham disc (Fig. 13c) and in more developed form on the Winchester disc (Fig. 13d). Group 2b comprises two Dover examples which while conforming to the basic pattern have a leaf and dot border in place of the running scroll. Group 2c comprises those examples which retain the border running scroll but which have a voided central element. This possibly originally contained an enamel. The Sutton Hoo, No. 3 escutcheon has been included in this group because it seems to be a schematized representation of the spirals on the Chesterton disc.

The Baginton bowl has an escutcheon which clearly falls into group 1. The same bowl, has a basal disc which belongs to group 2 (Fig. 13b). A predominant feature of group 2 is the running scroll and although some examples of group 2 are undoubtedly late the running scroll can be a very early motif in Germanic contexts. It occurs on late Roman metalwork from Vermand, for example, and in Britain on the early fifth century military buckle from Mucking.[59] In the late fifth-early sixth centuries it occurs on saucer brooches in an arrangement very similar to that of group 2 escutcheons. The motif did have a long currency, however, turning up in Pictland on the Dunichen symbol stone, for example, and in more elaborate form on the Aberlemno stone.[60] Later still, in the eighth century, from an Anglo-Saxon workshop, it occurs on the Bischofshofen cross.[61]

The large hanging-bowl from the Sutton Hoo 'ship burial' has escutcheons and discs which belong to Group 2a. These are set with red and blue enamel and millefiori glass and this bowl is probably the finest in the series. The bowl however, was old and patched when deposited and this should be taken into account when considering the date of its manufacture. The latest evidence seems to favour a date of c. 630 for the deposition of the grave goods which also include two smaller hanging bowls.[62]

The Whitby escutcheon (no. 3) may also be late in the series as the monastery at Whitby was not founded until 657.[63] The escutcheon is pierced for hanging as a pendant, however, and may have been very old when lost.

Despite the late character of many of the group 2 examples an early start to the series should not be excluded and this suggestion is reinforced by the two escutcheons and one disc from Dover. Kendrick has already suggested a Romanizing school producing these and other works in the fourth-fifth centuries[64] and while it is difficult to accept such an early dating for some of the other examples cited, such as the Lullingstone bowl, the leaf and dot arrangement on the Dover pieces does seem to be derived from Roman prototypes. A similar design to Dover No. 2 occurs on the, probably Roman, Newhaven House (Derbs.) disc and

Fig. 13

the zig-zag and dot occurs on early Germanic pottery and more significantly on Romano-Saxon pottery.[65]

An interesting feature of the Dover escutcheons is the central element on No. 2 and No. 3. Both seem to suggest a prototype 'Durrow spiral' while the intervening leaves on No. 3 are also reminiscent of the 'Durrow' pattern. The 'Durrow' triskele (N.B. four arms on the Dover pieces) is the predominant feature of group 4 and is traditionally dated to around the mid seventh century. However, one should beware of dating all examples of this type of ornamentation to the seventh century on the basis of the Book of Durrow. Durrow is the earliest illuminated manuscript to survive. Before Durrow, manuscript elaboration was chiefly in the form of decorated initial letters. When Durrow appears, the spiral patterns are in a mature form, the design had already been brought to almost rigid perfection. There are also many instances in the Book of Durrow where it is obvious that metalwork designs formed the prototypes for many of the elements. Colours copy those of contemporary enamels, for instance, and St. Matthew's robes look like millefiori or cloisonne enamelling.[66] This being the case, it is likely that the manuscript spirals copied the metalwork spirals rather than the other way around. On the other hand, it does not seem likely that out of date motifs would be copied and the 'Durrow spirals' must have been current at least until the second half of the seventh century. This is the more evident by the widespread occurrence of 'Durrow spirals' on class II Pictish symbol stones. We may assume then that the motif continued on metalwork into the second half of the seventh century but in a developed form which in no way precludes the currency of the motif at an earlier date or prejudices the suggestion that the Dover examples are late Roman.

Group 3. This group contains variations on a cross pattern on a circular disc as illustrated (see Fig. 14). The similarity of the designs on all the escutcheons and the association of the Kingston brooch with the Kingston bowl suggests a late sixth century date for this group.

Group 4. This is by far the largest group and is based on variations of the familiar 'developed trumpet pattern' or 'Durrow spirals' pattern. Many of the examples retain a striking adherence to this triskele pattern and there is little variation within the group (Fig. 15). Some examples, however, display not triskeles but a development of the Dover swastika. Sutton Hoo, No. 2, for example, has a zoomorphic swastika which suggests a link with group 4b. Group 4b seems to be associated with the ideas apparent in 4a and is characterized by interlaced animals.

It is difficult to arrive at any starting point for the Group 4 series but a possible late Roman date has already been suggested for the Group 2 Dover escutcheons and discs on which the beginnings of a spiral pattern can be seen and the fourth century openwork bronze from Verulamium is but one object which demonstrates that influences were apparent which could given an early start to the series.[67] The very great uniformity found in Group 4, however, suggests that the majority at least are contemporary and a few pointers regarding dating are here suggested.

That the 'Durrow spirals' motif was used on metalwork in the seventh-eighth centuries is clear from examples such as the Ardagh Chalice, the

Fig. 14

Fig. 15

Athlone Crucifixion Plaque and the Brechbennoch of St. Columba. Whether it was used on hanging-bowls after the mid-seventh century is another question. The distribution of group 4 bowls shows that they are virtually absent from Northumbria, with the exception of an anomalous, unprovenanced example, despite the fact that this group is widespread in southern England. The motif must have been introduced into Northumbria by craftsmen who reproduced on manuscript the metalwork forms with which they were familiar. The fact that almost no Northumbrian hanging-bowl bears a group 4 motif suggests that the hanging-bowl with circular escutcheon was going out of fashion by the mid-seventh century. It is probable however that the hanging-bowl with oblong escutcheons continued in use and it is interesting to note that the one group 4 disc which can be dated to the late seventh century, the repousse plate from St. Ninian's Isle, occurs on a bowl which has unused oblong escutcheons.[68] This disc is secondary to the bowl but does seem to have been old itself when used for this purpose. The hanging-bowl 'per se' does seem to have been in decline during the second half of the seventh century and although the series continued in Ireland to a later date no mainland British bowl can be certainly dated later than the seventh century.

On the other hand two Group 4a bowls are known from warrior graves dated to at least seventh century and the Group 4b escutcheon from Benty Grange could also be late. The Lowbury Hill bowl is associated with a leaf-shaped spearhead (C2) and a curved cone sugar-loaf shield boss.[69] Sugar-loaf shield bosses seem to be a development of the seventh century and, more particularly, to be increasingly common in the second half of the seventh century.[70] The Winchester Bowl is associated with a seax which is certainly seventh century. Furthermore the Winchester bowl is in very good condition and the Lowbury Hill bowl is in reasonable condition compared with some examples. Benty Grange is sometimes claimed as a Christian burial on the basis of the silver crosses on the helmet and leather cup. This would place it in the second half of the seventh century. This is the date favoured by Bruce-Mitford for the burial and in the same article he draws attention to the similarity between the creatures on the fragmentary escutcheons and those of the 'IN' monogram from St. John in the Durham Cathedral A II 10 manuscript. The Benty Grange hanging-bowl, therefore, is not likely to have been made much before the middle of the seventh century.[71]

The Lullingstone bowl is representative of Group 4 and at Caenby fragments of a 'double-axe' motif attached to a circular plate and ornamented with three strand interlace is very reminiscent of the Lullingstone escutcheons.[72] Associated with the Caenby burial is a tapering plate in a style described by Wilson as a fusion between Style I and Style II.[73] He is here talking about one of the Taplow horn-mounts but the resemblance between the Taplow and Caenby pieces is considerable. A date for the introduction of Style II into England is still a debateable point but late sixth/early seventh century seems reasonable for the 'fusion style'. By analogy with Caenby, late sixth century/early seventh may be suggested for the Lullingstone bowl. Moulds with three-strand closely spaced interlace resembling the Caenby and Lullingstone interlace occur at the Mote of Mark - although it should be noted that Caenby is animal interlace whereas the Mote of Mark is not. Recent excavations indicate that this site

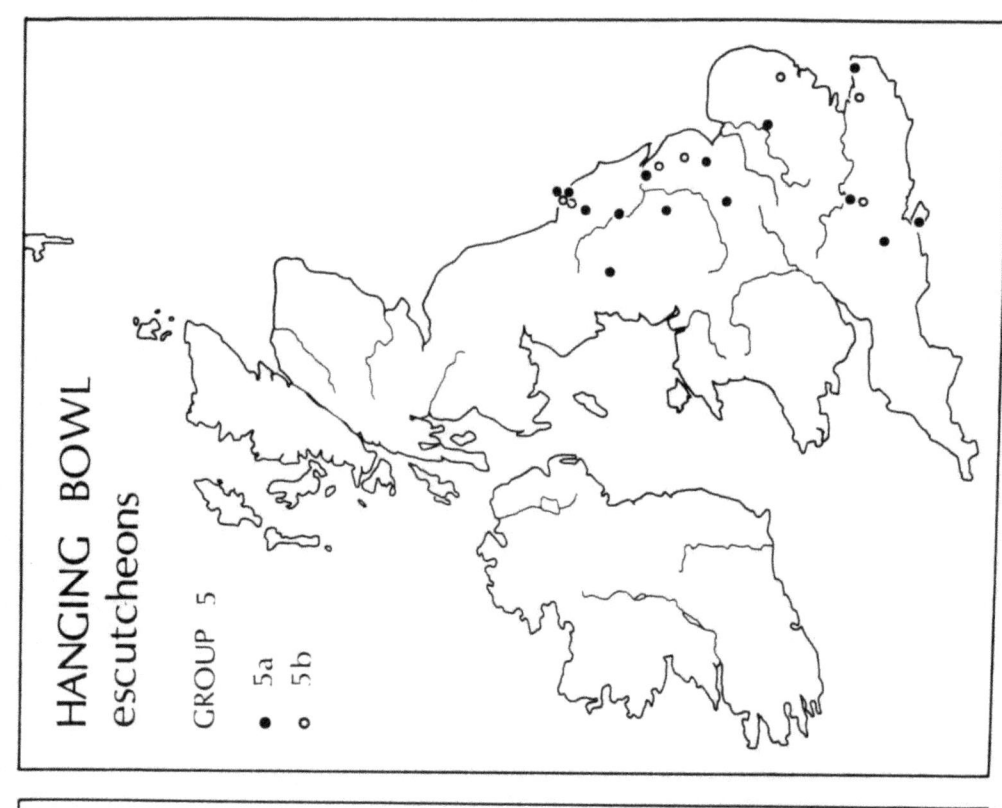

Fig. 17

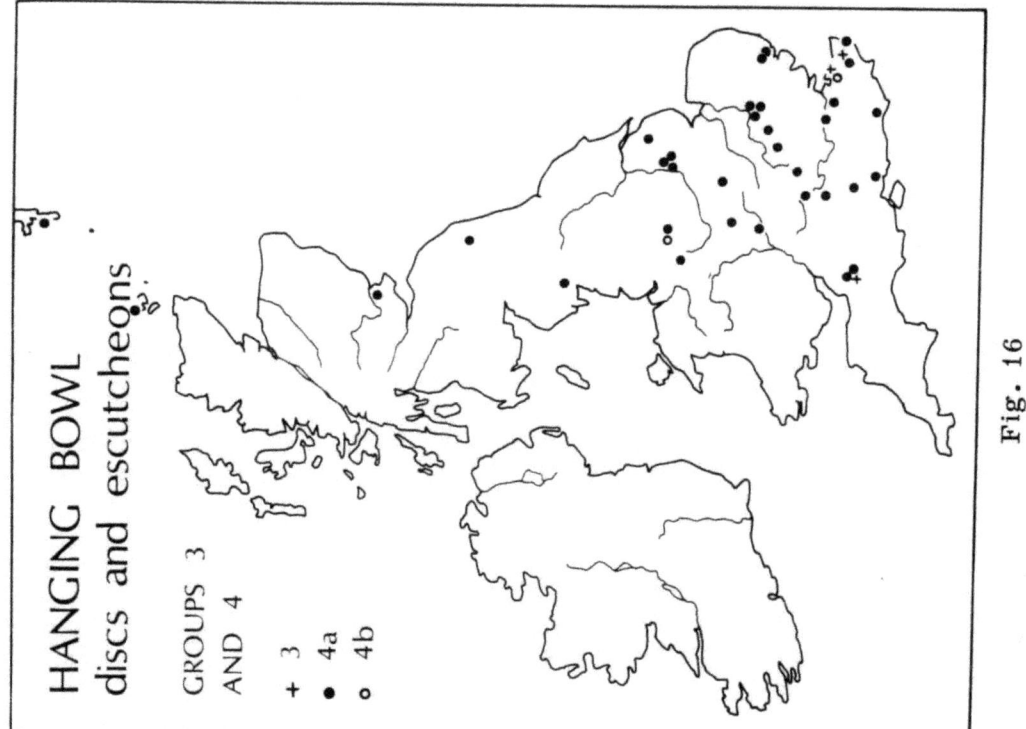

Fig. 16

was destroyed early in the seventh century with occupation in the fifth and sixth. On the basis of these examples one would like to date the majority of Group 4 escutcheons to the period from the late sixth century to the mid-seventh.

Group 5. This group is characterised by all those escutcheons of triangular or ovoid shape. 5a includes all the plain versions of this type including those with bulbs at the base of the escutcheon. 5b includes all the decorated examples of this type including those with triangular or pelta-like appendages (birds' tails).

Two bowls of group 5 can be dated by their association in graves. The Ford Down bowl was associated with two leaf-shaped spearheads (C3), a sugar loaf shield boss, an iron buckle with three garnets 'en cabochon' and a seax and sheath fittings. Style II decoration on the pommel and the bird-figure at the tip of the sheath confirm a seventh century date for the seax while the sugar-loaf shield boss suggests that the grave may be as late as the second half of the seventh century.[74] The bowl from Barton on Humber is dated to the seventh century on the basis of an interlace disc associated with the bowl in a ? female burial.[75] Again, this burial may be as late as the mid seventh century. The studded interlace on the disc resembles that of the great buckle from Sutton Hoo, however, although the Barton disc has a tighter arrangement and a very similar interlace is to be found on some of the 'fusion style' drinking horn mounts from Taplow. Closely spaced three-strand interlace similar to that on the Caenby pieces, suggested as a parallel by Vierck, was being manufactured at the Mote of Mark in the late sixth-early seventh century.[76] It is conceivable, then, that this grave belongs to the first half of the seventh century.

Two of the Whitby examples belong to group 5a while two others belong to 5b. These could possibly date to the second half of the seventh century while one escutcheon (Fig. 18, j) has triquetra decoration which may be as late as the eighth or ninth centuries.

The Benniworth escutcheon has a group 4 motif (Fig. 18, h) adapted to fit the inverted pear shape and should be dated accordingly.

The Faversham (Fig. 18, f) and Needham Market escutcheons have a similar decoration of triskeles and spirals but the Faversham example is not identical. From what can be seen of the Needham Market escutcheon and the central element of the Needham Market disc, however, these should also be dated with the Benniworth example.

Nearly all these 5b escutcheons have, or did have, pelta or triangular shaped 'tails'. A few of the plain examples had a similar bulb at the base of the escutcheon (e.g. Fig. 18, b).

The two Finningley bowls both have the inbent rim form which Kendrick considered was a continuation of the late fourth century Irchester type of bowl while at Sleaford in Lincolnshire is another bowl with inbent rim and outward facing bird's head terminals (Fig. 18, g).[77] The Chessel Down example has this early rim. It may be possible that the situation here is one of development from a late fourth century type represented by the Sleaford bowl, acquiring

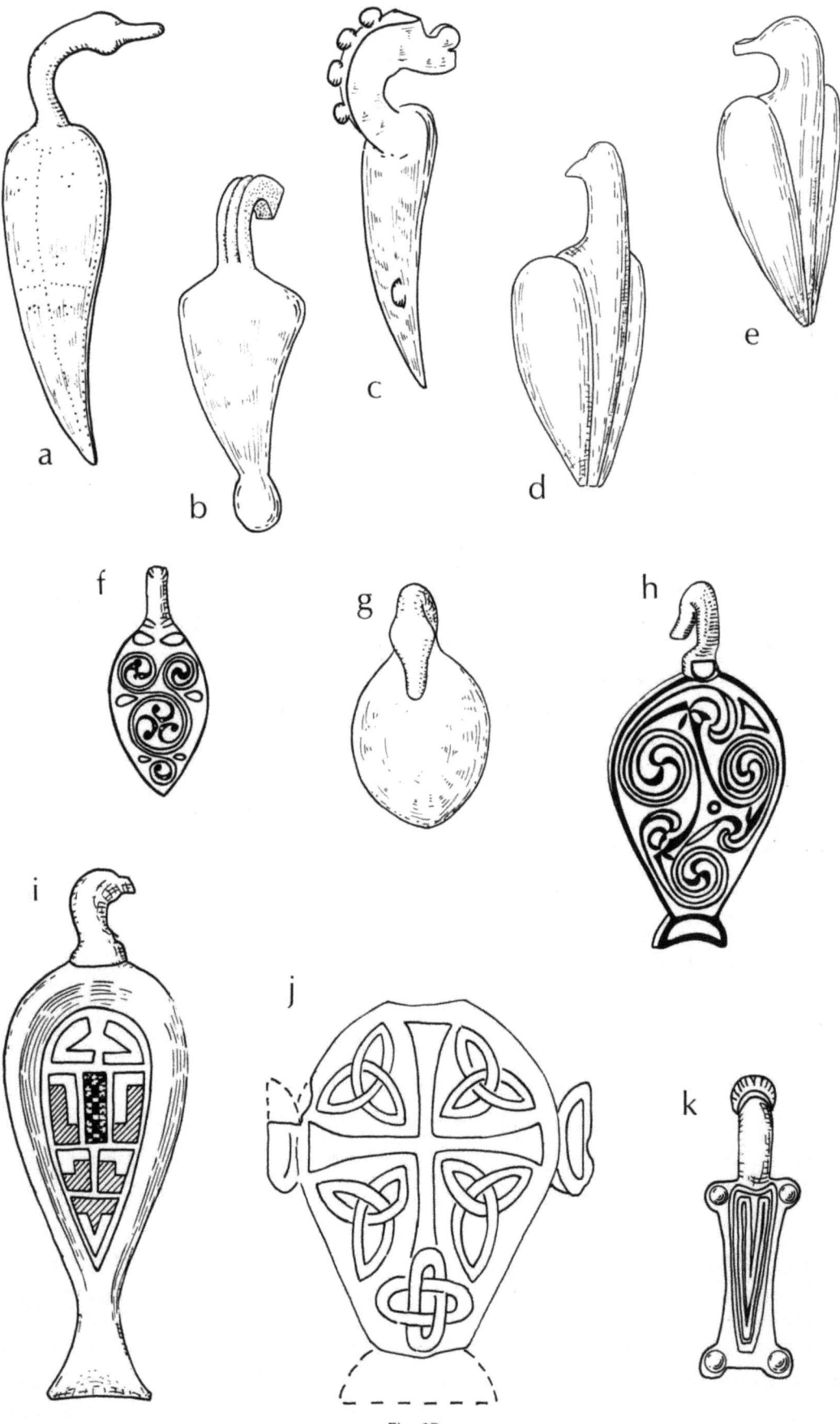

Fig. 18

elaboration in the form of a bulb at the base of the escutcheon, while the plain type continued, itself developing a stronger bowl rim and larger escutcheons. The tailed type was further elaborated, probably in the second half of the sixth century, by spiral ornament and the resolution of the bulb into a triangular tail. Whitby No. 2 would appear to be the latest British example of this series. It probably had a tail but this is now missing. The bowl cannot have been deposited at Whitby before the second half of the seventh century and it may even be later than this. The Hawnby bowl with its very long terminals and folded-over rim must also be late. The punched dot decoration is disconcertingly reminiscent of the silver bowl, No. 1, from St. Ninian's Isle.[78]

It looks, in fact, as though group 5 is a very long running series. It possibly comprises some of the earliest and some of the latest of all hanging-bowls. The greatest concentration of group 5 examples - representing fifteen bowls - occurs in the Yorkshire/Lincolnshire area and it is likely that the group 5 escutcheon remained popular in this area throughout the currency of the hanging-bowl. Possibly the earliest examples owe a lot to continental influence during the Roman period. Bowls from Barton (Fig. 18d) and Silchester can be paralleled at Naunheim and Sackrau.[79] The Sleaford type on the other hand probably represents a native attempt to convert an Irchester type bowl into a hanging-bowl. A fusion of the two groups produced the standard group 5 escutcheon in the south in the late Roman/sub-Roman period (e.g. Chessel Down and Sarre) while further north the same development was taking place, although still retaining outbent hooks at Arncliffe with Whitby No. 2 probably representing the last stage in the development of group 5 on mainland Britain.

Irish and Continental contexts

The elongated escutcheon, often bird shaped, seems to have had a continued existence in Ireland however. Many of the later examples come from Viking graves in Norway and Sweden and it seems best to regard these as loot from Ireland rather than Britain (Fig. 18, i). Earlier hanging-bowls were not unknown in Ireland - a group 1 escutcheon was found in the river Bann. Furthermore, while British hanging-bowls seem to be uniformly hemispherical and in the great majority of cases in bronze, Irish bowls are known in wood, stone and metal and in hemispherical, oval and triangular shapes.[80] Thus, it might be argued, the hanging-bowl was a common vessel in Ireland were it not for the fact that so few Irish examples have survived. Those that have survived seem in general to be later than the British series, the Ballinderry No. 1 'hanging-lamp', for example, is possibly as late as the early eleventh century.[81] Although the practice in Christian Ireland of not burying grave goods with the dead has no doubt greatly reduced the number of survivals it is, nevertheless, unlikely that the hanging-bowl can have been very common in Ireland. If the River Bann escutcheon is accepted as an outlier of the Scottish group 1 series (Fig. 11) then this again reduces the number of early examples and, as seems to have been the case with type F and type H penannular brooches, the Irish hanging-bowl series seems to have been a development and elaboration of a mainland British metalwork type, which continues beyond the currency of the mainland type.[82]

A small number of circular escutcheons do occur in Norwegian contexts but these have a decidedly 'late' appearance bearing little resemblance to the British series. They do, however, seem to reflect contemporary trends in Irish metalwork (see Henry 1936, pls. XXXVI and XXXVII). Of more immediate consequence are the continental examples occurring outside Norwegian graves. Dr. Vierck has argued that the development of hanging bowls is intimately connected with the history of the Church from its Roman beginnings to its development in the Anglo Saxon period.[83] In support of this argument he cites the occurrence of escutcheon finds on the continent associating them with nearby centres of insular missionary activity. While the evidence will not allow an exclusive, or even predominant, use of hanging bowls by the church it is conceivable that once established, ecclesiastical conservatism perpetuated their employment after their use had been discontinued in a secular context. This might account for the continental finds and also shed light on the late associations at Whitby and St. Ninian's Isle. With regard to the continental examples the only one which really seems to fit into the British series is the disc from Lede.[84] This is pierced presumably for hanging as a pendant and may not have reached Lede on a hanging-bowl. The unassociated disc from Kaiseraugst is also superficially similar to the Group 4a series but has been described as a Merovingian copy of an Irish model. Dr. Vierck sees the escutcheon from Impfingen as deriving from eighth century Northumbria.[85] As a stage in the development from the group 5 escutcheons to the later anthropomorphic Irish examples (as seen on the Miklebostad bowl) this explanation fits very well.

Rim Form

Mention has been made of certain 'early' and 'late' rim forms. The development of the rim form is a point that has been made by a number of writers on the subject.[86] Essentially the development on mainland Britain is from the inbent rim of the Sleaford and Chessel Down bowls (Fig. 19 c) to the folded-over rim of the Winchester and Hawnby bowls (Fig. 19, h and i). Very early on in this development it would seem that the inbent rim was thickened, by hammering, although still in some cases retaining the original profile (as at Baginton) (Fig. 19, d). This development would seem to be borne out by the dated examples. Group 4, furthermore, a late group of relatively short duration, has by far the largest proportion of fold-over rims to hammered rims whereas group 1, argued as essentially early, has a very high ratio of hammered rims. The other groups are fairly evenly divided. (In fig. 19 the outer circle represents the total number of possible bowls in each group. Most finds are of stray escutcheons, however, and the inner circle represents the number of actual bowls in each group - measured across the diameter - differentiated by their rim form.)

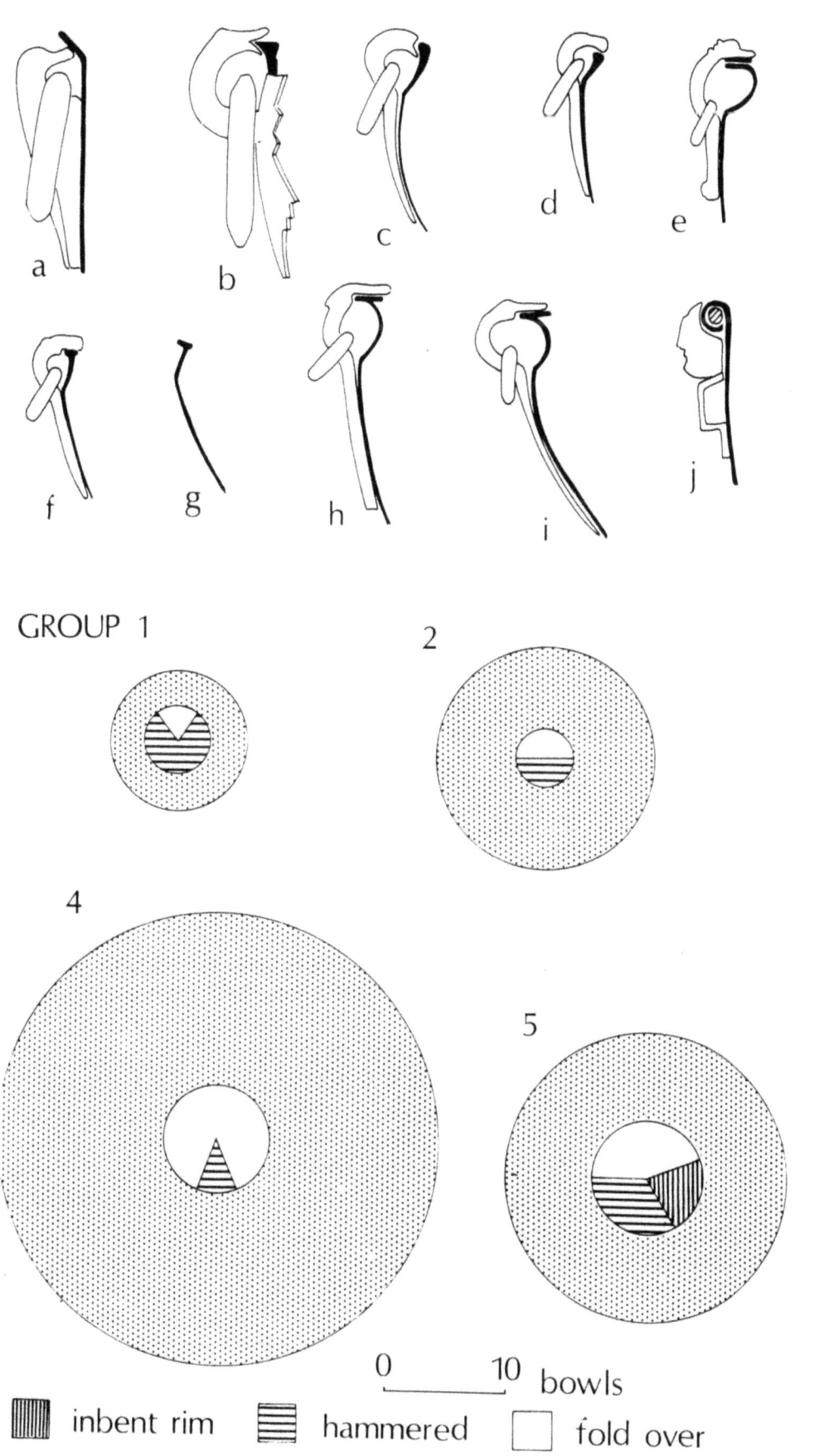

Fig. 19: Hanging-bowl rim forms.

CONCLUSIONS

The Dark Age hanging-bowl sequence is a product, firstly, of influences coming in from the continent in the late Roman period, seen in the Silchester and Barton (Cambs.) bowls. Developing from this are native attempts to produce similar bowls by adding escutcheons to already existing types of bowl.

The functional aspect of hanging-bowls, though much discussed, has sometimes been dismissed as of little relevance to the real 'problem'. The Irchester bowls may have belonged to some sort of wine serving kit - a strainer is associated with the hoard and the possibility of a post-Roman use in serving or mixing wine has been discussed above. Dr. Vierck has shown how Roman tripod stands with their bowls may have served as the prototype for the series and how the possibility of a variety of uses should not be excluded.[87] In particular it would seem that, at least in the later period, an association with the Church should not be ruled out. Furthermore, one is also tempted to wonder whether the very thin bronze bowls with single zoomorphic escutcheons and loose rings, typified by the Rose Ash and Youlton finds, can have played any part in the development. There is admittedly a huge chronological void between the late first century B.C./early first century A.D. of these bowls and the hanging bowl series but examples such as the ox-head from Welshpool and the bucket mount from Mount Sorrel are beginning to bridge the gap in the continuity of the western metal working tradition.[88] It is interesting to note that a bowl, comparable with the one from Rose Ash, coming from Poland, has a zoomorphic spout equipped with a strainer (for wine?).[89] Is it possible that the strainer on the Ballinderry 'hanging lamp' served a similar purpose?

Distribution of the early bowls is, in general, in the south and east. During the fifth century development seems to have proceeded in more or less the same areas with the exception that the openwork series is introduced into the north of Scotland. At first this presents a problem in that all the escutcheons of group 1a and 1b are very similar yet there is nothing as yet to bridge the large gap between the southern and the northern examples. Contact must have taken place, however, and the context may be suggested by the distribution of H penannular brooches (Fig. 8). It has already been suggested that the H brooches in Germanic contexts on the East Coast of England represent links with Pictland in the fifth and sixth centuries. They may, of course, have been lost by Pictish raiders but in either case it seems possible that hanging-bowls made this a two-way affair. The approximate contemporaneity of H brooches and group 1 hanging-bowls is attested by their presence together in the Tummel Bridge hoard.[90] As regards the direction in which these influences appear to have been flowing it has been suggested that the H brooches originate in Scotland. Hanging-bowls, on the other hand, could possibly have been in use in Pictland at this time but it seems preferable to regard group 1 as originating in England out of Romano-British openwork plaques such as the Richborough and Leicester ones. The Baginton bowl has been dated to the seventh century.[91] The inturned rim could conceivably be described as an early type, however, and a basal disc has a running scroll border with a central marigold reminiscent of Dover

No. 1 for which an early date has already been suggested (Fig. 13a and b). Furthermore the star elements on the escutcheon are very reminiscent of the 'eyes' which are a recurrent feature of IIA buckles. If the Baginton bowl is not a survival in a late context then the possibility remains that it is based on earlier prototypes. The Tummel Bridge and Castle Tioram bowls both have what Fowler has defined as 'later' rims so all in all a prior development in the south seems likely. Nevertheless the group 1 mould from Craig Phadrig shows that Pictland was not only trading in bowls but also producing its own.[92]

At some point, probably in the second half of the fifth century, group 2 begins to develop. The Dover escutcheons are most likely the earliest and, as the greatest concentration of group 2 escutcheons is to be found in Kent, this again indicates an origin in this region. Group 2 distribution is primarily up the East Coast and this fact is interesting in that it again indicates an exchange of influences probably seaborne along the East Coast, albeit the few examples are spread over a century and a half.

By the second half of the sixth century group 4 had begun to develop as had probably the decorated examples of the ovoid group 5. By far the largest number of escutcheons are in group 4 yet, excluding the exceptional St. Ninian's Isle disc, this group seems to have had the shortest currency. An escutcheon (unpublished) has been has been found at Clatchard's Craig and in view of the suggested dating of group 4 and the absence of group 4 escutcheons from Northumbria, the escutcheon from Westmorland should probably also be assigned a Celtic provenance. If most of the bowls are found in Anglo-Saxon contexts and it is difficult to believe that all the bowls are imports from the Celtic areas then the alternative explanation is equally difficult to justify. Whereas, for the other groups, prototype designs may be looked for in Roman and sub-Roman Britain (and a development of these groups within the Anglo-Saxon areas seems plausible) if there is any connexion between group 4 escutcheons and such pieces as the Verulamium bronze and the central element of the Dover escutcheons then this development must be looked for in the Celtic and Pictish kingdoms of the west and north. In view of the example from Clatchard's Craig and the applied animals on the Lullingstone bowl then, bearing in mind the similar appliques on the Hildersham bowl with its group 1 escutcheons and the fact that a mould for a group 1 escutcheon comes from Craig Phadrig, Pictland would seem to be the most likely home for group 4 in its initial stages or at least the home of the craftsmen who produced the bowls with group 4 enamelled escutcheons.

By the mid-seventh century, it is suggested, the hanging-bowl was in decline, at least in mainland Britain. A certain number of examples can be found to post-date this but they must represent the last fling of the hanging-bowl tradition, at least in secular use. There is, however, always the very great possibility that the evidence for the last stages described has been severely distorted by the advent of Christianity and the decline in the practice of placing grave goods with the dead. However this may be, one would still expect some evidence in one form or another. The latest bowls in the series, on present evidence, are possibly four from Whtiby, the St. Ninian's Isle bowl, possibly the Winchester and Ipswich bowls and the Witham bowl. All are coastal sites, or at least accessible by sea, and a Northumbrian origin has been suggested for the St. Ninian's Isle bowl. A common source for all these late bowls is probably not likely but a common influence may be suggested at a time when the hanging-bowl was rapidly going out of fashion. Not all these bowls are necessarily late, in particular the Ipswich and Winchester bowls need not be, but once again it does seem as though the East Coast route is the means behind a dissemination of influence.

Throughout this discussion of bowls and brooches stress has been laid on the importance of seaborne traffic down the east and west Coasts of mainland Britain and the links between Ireland and western Britain. This is to some extent mirrored by the distribution of imported pottery of classes A, B, D, and E which has, however, up to now, been almost entirely confined to Celtic sites.[93] It has been suggested that this is perhaps due to the influence of the Celtic Church which certainly had the Mediterranean connexions to organise such a trade. But this is not an entirely satisfactory explanation, especially in respect of the profit motive, and besides E ware does not come from the Mediterranean. Perhaps future work will extend the imported pottery distribution into the Anglo-Saxon areas as well.

At this point a note of caution should be sounded about the loose use of the word trade especially when such a small number of objects are involved, spread over a considerable period of time. Nevertheless although connexions may have been sporadic at best and due as much to individual migratory craftsmen as to trade as such, the pattern of coast-wise connexions exists and ignores apparent cultural boundaries. Certainly not all the 'Celtic' objects in Anglo-Saxon graves can be put down to raiding.

The sub-Roman period saw the native population of Britain subjected to the incursions of newcomers from practically every side. The problem of the fate of these original inhabitants, however, is thought to be a problem only in the English area. The reason for this may be that on the one hand archaeological evidence is scarce for the Celtic areas during this period, and what evidence there is, serves only to demonstrate their cultural unity at this time. No great change therefore is indicated in the archaeological record. On the however, the evidence seems to indicate vast changes and this must be due in part to a clash of culture that was not met with in the west. That is to say the largely un-Romanized highland zone was able to absorb incomers possessing a similar barbarian culture without major upheaval, and this only serves to emphasize the changes which took place in the Romanized lowland zone. How true this picture is is difficult to assess but there are indications that it may be questioned on some important aspects. It was suggested above that Romano-Saxon pottery and certain 'British' groups of military buckle are two manifestations of a trend in the late Roman period which shows a willingness to adopt Germanic elements of design. In the case of the pottery this is clear enough and certainly the buckles do owe their inspiration to continental influence which _may_ have been introduced into Britain by Germanic mercenaries in the 4th century. It is equally likely, however, that the same trends which led to this particular late Roman metalwork style on the contenent (e.g. at Vermand) were also present in Britain and is seen in fact on pieces in the Coleraine hoard (Fig. 13e). It is a general late Roman provincial style and not specifically Germanic in its roots although it was adopted and adapted by Germans. In this context and bearing in mind the early presence of

Germans in Britain the metalwork of late Roman Britain can lay a strong claim to a fair share of the influence behind many of the pieces traditionally labelled Anglo-Saxon. Leeds long ago pointed out the significance of the penannular brooches in Anglo-Saxon contexts and it is suggested above that the flat annular developed out of the penannular in order to provide a field for the style of metalwork decoration current at this time. Leeds illustrates three brooches which show well the sort of development which was taking place.[94] The annular brooches are just one element in the metalworking repertoire of the Anglo-Saxon that display its Romano-British background in form and style. Furthermore, one finds it difficult to accept Haseloff's proposition that no Celtic influence on English ornament antedates Irish missionary activities beginning in 634.[95] Apart from the considerable influence on metalwork exerted by the native British in the English areas, contact with the outside Celtic world must surely have been continuous. Without going into detail the parallel development of interlace in the Celtic West and Anglo-Saxon East may be cited. Although it is possible, and likely, that interlace reached the two areas independently - via the continent to Anglo-Saxon England and direct from the Mediterranean to the Celtic West - it is hard to believe that no cross fertilization between the two areas took place. The similarities between the Mote of Mark interlace and that of the Lullingstone bowl has already been noted as have the arguments for dating it $\underline{c}$. 600. The opposing beasts heads on the Alfriston brooch have already been mentioned and more than likely represent influence from contemporary 'Celtic' F penannulars. Similarly if it is accepted that a late development of the Celtic ox-protome influenced the F series then it is also possible that a similar influence can be seen at work on the zoomorphic feet of certain cruciform brooches. One from Lyminge (Fig. 4a) is particularly reminiscent of the ox-head mounts whereas an example in the Corbridge Museum seems to have more in common with the brooch development. It is not suggested that these cruciform brooches are influenced directly by imported penannulars or bucket mounts but rather, and more significantly, that the name influences were available to the makers of both the Celtic and the Anglo-Saxon brooches, and that the already zoomorphic foot of the cruciform brooch was re-interpreted accordingly. Some F penannulars do occur in Anglo-Saxon graves and so do a larger number of type G. The type G examples are significantly distributed along a hypothetical border line. However the F and G examples found their way into 'Anglo-Saxon' graves - either by trade, plunder or errant craftsmen - the type H penannulars along the east coast, whether initially lost by Pictish raiders or representative of some more positive contact, similarly demonstrate the way in which influence could be transmitted across apparent cultural boundaries. This interpretation is strengthened by the occurrence of group 1 hanging-bowls in Pictland. Although the Craig Phadrig mould shows that these bowls were being produced in Pictland, it is suggested that the influence is from the South.

In conclusion, then, it would appear from a study of a limited field of material that there is evidence to suggest, on the one hand, a survival of probably the basis of the late Roman population in the English area, evidenced by the distribution of native British penannular types and the continuation of Late Roman motifs on metalwork. On the other hand there would also seem to be a certain amount, certainly not negligible, of contact between the various cultural areas of Britain at this time and with this the transmission of influences. This essay has been concerned primarily with two series of metalwork objects but these must surely represent but one element in a larger pattern of movement to and fro between cultural areas. This fact has always been accepted with regard to the Celtic West and one feels that the Anglo-Saxons should also be included within this pattern.

APPENDIX

Escutcheons and discs grouped by type. A number following a name differentiates bowls from the same locality while a letter following a name and number differentiates dissimilar escutcheons or discs on a common bowl.

Group 1 (figs. 10 and 11)   Illustrated

1a Baginton, No. 1a (4 escutcheons)   (fig. 10, c)
    River Bann (escutcheon)   (Henry, 1956, p. 80)
    Castle Tioram (escutcheon)   (fig. 10, b)
    Craig Phadrig (mould)   (described in Stevenson, 1973)
    Eastwell (escutcheon)   (Med. Arch., 1964, pl. 19c)
    Hildersham (3 escutcheons)   (fig. 10, a)
    West Wickham

1b Tummel Bridge (escutcheon)   (fig. 10, e)
    Wilton (4 escutcheons)   (fig. 10, d)

1c Eastry (escutcheon)   (fig. 10, f)
    Faversham No. 1 (3 escutcheons)   (fig. 10, g)

Group 2 (figs. 12 and 13)

2a Baginton, No. 1b (disc)   (fig. 13, b)
    Bekesbourne, No. 1b (disc)   (Haselhoff, 1958, pl. VII)
    Dover, No. 1a (escutcheon)   (fig. 13, a)
    Faversham, No. 3a (disc)   (fig. 13, c)
    Ipswich (disc)   (Wilson, 1973, pl. XLIX, c)
    Needham Market, No. 1a (disc)   (Henry, 1936)
    Sutton Hoo, No. 1 (escutcheons and   (Bruce-Mitford, 1973, pls.
        discs)   8 and 9)
    Winchester, No. 1b (disc)   (fig. 13, d)

2b Dover, No. 1b (escutcheon)   (fig. 13, f)
    Dover, No. 1c (disc)   (fig. 13, e)

2c Barlaston, No. 1b (disc)   (Henry, 1936)
    Bekesbourne, No. 1a (escutcheon)   (Haselhoff, 1958, pl. VII)
    British Museum (escutcheon)   ("   "   "   ")
    Capheaton (3 escutcheons)   (Henry, 1936)
    Chesterton on Fossway No. 1b (disc)   ("   ")
    Sutton Hoo, No. 3 (escutcheon)   (Bruce-Mitford, 1973, pl. 24b)
    Whitby, No. 3 (escutcheon)   (fig. 13, g)

Group 3 (figs 14 and 16)

    Camerton, No. 3 (escutcheon)   (fig. 14, a)
    Faversham, No. 2 (3 escutcheons)   (fig. 14, b)
    Kingston, No. 1a (3 escutcheons)   (Kendrick, 1932)
    Kingston, No. 1b (disc)   (fig. 14, c)

Group 4 (figs. 15 and 16)

4a	Barlaston, No. 1a (escutcheon)	(Henry, 1936)
	Barrington, No. 1 (escutcheon)	(fig. 15, d)
	Barrington, No. 2 (disc)	(Henry, 1936)
	Birsay (mould)	(unpublished)
	Camerton, No. 1 (escutcheon)	(fig. 15f)
	Camerton, No. 2 (escutcheon)	(Henry, 1936)
	Chalton (basal disc)	(Med. Arch., XVII, pl. VI)
	Chesterton on Fossway No. 1a (4 escutcheons)	(fig. 15, b)
	Clatchard's Craig (escutcheon)	(unpublished)
	Dover, No. 2 (escutcheon)	(Henry, 1936)
	Greenwich (3 escutcheons)	(Henry, 1936)
	Hildersham, No. 1b (disc)	(D.A.B., fig. 23, b)
	Hitchin (escutcheon)	(fig. 15, a)
	Keythorpe Common (3 escutcheons)	(lost)
	Kingston, No. 2 (escutcheon)	(fig. 15, h)
	Loveden Hill, No. 1 (3 escutcheons)	(Med. Arch., 1960)
	Loveden Hill, No. 2 (escutcheon)	(Med. Arch., 1960)
	Loveden Hill, No. 3 (escutcheon)	(Med. Arch., 1960)
	Loveden Hill, No. 4 (3 escutcheons and disc)	(Med. Arch., 1960)
	Lowbury Hill, (3 escutcheons)	(Kilbride-Jones, 1936-7)
	Lullingstone (4 escutcheons)	(fig. 15, c)
	Market Rasen (escutcheon)	(?)
	Middleton Moor, No. 1 (escutcheon)	(Henry, 1936)
	Northumberland (3 escutcheons and disc)	(Kendrick, 1932)
	Oving (escutcheon)	(fig. 15, e)
	Oxford (escutcheon)	(Henry, 1936)
	St. Ninian's Isle (exterior basal disc)	(Wilson, 1973, pl. XXV, b)
	Stoke Golding, No. 1 (escutcheon)	(fig. 15, g)
	Stoke Golding, No. 2 (escutcheon)	(fig. 15, i)
	Sutton Hoo No. 2 (disc)	(Bruce-Mitford, 1973, pl. 24a)
	Totternhoe (escutcheon)	(?)
	Victoria and Albert Museum (escutcheon)	(Henry, 1936)
	Winchester No. 1a (3 escutcheons)	(Kilbride-Jones, 1936-7)
4b	Benty Grange, No. 1 (escutcheon)	(fig. 14 j)
	Faversham, No. 4a (disc)	(fig. 14 i)
	Faversham, No. 4b (disc)	(Kendrick, 1932)

Group 5 (figs. 17 and 18)

5a	Arncliffe Cave (escutcheon)	(Henry, 1936)
	Barton, No. 1 (escutcheon)	(fig. 18, d)
	Barton, Lincs. (3 escutcheons)	(Capelle and Vierck, 1971, fig. 13)
	Chessel Down (3 escutcheons)	(fig. 18, b)
	Finningley, Nos. 1 & 2 (3 escutcheons)	(fig. 18, c)
	Ford Down (3 escutcheons)	(Musty, 1969)
	Hawnby (3 escutcheons)	(fig. 18 a)

	Sarre (escutcheon)	(Henry, 1936)
	Silchester (escutcheon)	(Henry, 1936)
	Sleaford (4 escutcheons)	(fig. 18, g)
	Twyford (2 escutcheons)	(Henry, 1936)
	Whitby, No. 4 (escutcheon)	(Peers and Radford, 1943)
	Whitby, No. 5 (escutcheon)	(Peers and Radford, 1943)
	York, Castle Yard (3 escutcheons)	(Henry, 1936)
5b	Basingstoke (3 escutcheons)	(Henry, 1936)
	Benniworth (escutcheon)	(fig. 18, h)
	Faversham, No. 3b (escutcheon)	(fig. 18 f)
	Manton Common (3 escutcheons)	
	Needham Market, No. 1b (escutcheon)	(Henry, 1936)
	Whitby, No. 1	(fig. 18, j)
	Whitby, No. 2	(Haselhoff, 1958, pl. VII)

Miscellaneous Group

Barton (Mildenhall)(escutcheon and discs)	(Henry, 1936)
Caistor (3 escutcheons)	(Kendrick, 1932)
Grindlow (bowl only)	(Ozanne, 1962, fig. 9a)
St. Ninian's Isle (escutcheons)	(Wilson, 1973, pl. XXV, b)
White Horse Hill (disc)	(Henry, 1936)
Witham (escutcheons and disc)	(Wilson, 1973, pl. LI)
York, Castle Yard (base plate)	(Henry, 1936)

There are a number of discs and escutcheons which do not fit into any of the above defined groups although some decorative elements on them may relate to elements present on the grouped discs and escutcheons. These have been included under a miscellaneous group for the sake of completeness and have been considered where appropriate.

REFERENCES

1. Leeds, 1936, pl. 1.
2. Alcock, 1971, fig. 31.
3. Panegyrici Latini, VIII, (V) 16, 2; Frere, 1967, p. 346.
4. Myres, 1956.
5. Myres, 1969.
6. Myres, 1969, pp. 62-83.
7. Hawkes and Dunning, 1961.
8. Hawkes, 1974.
9. Ibid., p. 393. See also Hawkes, 1972 and Hawkes, 1972a.
10. Evison, 1965.
11. Evison, 1968.
12. 'West Stow', C.A. 40; Med. Arch. XIII, 1969.
13. 'Chalton', C.A. 37, pp. 55-61.
14. Kilbride-Jones, 1935-6 and 1935-7; Savory, 1956; Fowler, 1963.
15. Leeds, 1945.
16. Fowler, 1963, p. 114.
17. Ibid., p. 101.
18. Ibid., p. 103. Freestone Hill; Raftery, P.R.I.A., 1969, p. 62, fig. 19.
19. Proc. Camb. Antiq. Soc., XLVII (1953), p.25f (fig.4). Rose Ash; Fox, 1961.
20. Alcock, 1963.
21. Hawkes, 1951, p.172-199.
22. Dinorben; Gardner and Savory, 1964, fig.21. Twyford; Hawkes, 1951, p.1. IX.
23. Gardner and Savory, 1964, pp.145-6.
24. Ham Hill and Dinorben (1912) escutcheons illustrated in Hawkes, 1951, pl. VII, 1, 2.
25. Kilbride-Jones, 1935-7, no. 87 (admittedly a poor example).
26. Kilbride-Jones, 1937, illustrates many of the Irish examples.
27. Wainwright, 1955, p. 111.
28. Curle, 1913.
29. Laing, 1973, p. 121-5.

30. Fowler, 1963, p. 111.
31. Thomas, 1959.
32. Ibid.
33. Fowler, 1963, p. 111.
34. Frere, 1967, p. 377.
35. E.g. Croy and Loch Fyne; Wilson, 1973, pls. XXXVIII, a and XLI, c.
36. Curle, 1913 illustrates a cast from the mould.
37. Laing, 1973, p. 121-5.
38. Fowler, 1963, p. 113.
39. E.g. Curle, 1913, pl. 14/8.
40. Fowler, 1963, pp. 101-2.
41. Skye brooch illustrated in P.S.A.S., vol. LXXXVII? 1952-3, pl. XXIX.
42. Thomas, 1959; Peacock and Thomas, 1967.
43. Mote of Mark; Curle, 1913. Dinas Powys; Alcock, 1963.
44. Kendrick, 1932; Henry, 1936; Kilbride-Jones, 1936-7; Fowler, 1968.
45. E.g. Camerton - see fig. 3a.
46. Vierck, 1970.
47. Vierck, 1970a.
48. Bruce-Mitford, 1972; Fennel, 1960.
49. Gresham, 1942, p. 254; Vierck, 1970, p. 24-5.
50. Davidson and Webster, 1967.
51. Musty, 1969, fig. 4, e.
52. Vierck, 1970, pl. IX; fig. 12, 2; Musty, 1969, fig. 4, e.
53. Ibid, fig. 71, 1 and 2.
54. Ozanne, 1962, p. 22.
55. Haseloff, 1958, p. 89-90.
56. Thomas, 1961, especially fig. 13.
57. Hawkes and Dunning, 1961.
58. Wheeler, 1932a, no. 101: p. 86, nos. 130 and 133: p. 90.
59. Vermand; P. Lasko, 'The Kingdom of the Franks', London, 1971, fig. 4. Muching; Antiq. J. XLVII, 1968.
60. Dunnichen: E.C.P.M.S., pl. 2; Aberlemno: E.C.P.M.S., pl. 9.
61. Lasko, op. cit., fig. 120.

62. Bruce-Mitford, 1972, pp. 54-9.
63. Bede, III, 24.
64. Kendrick, 1932, p.169f.
65. Newhaven House disc: Ozanne, 1962-3, fig. 15, b.
66. See for example Thomas, 1971, ill. 80.
67. Wheeler, 1932, p.300.
68. Wilson, 1973.
69. Evison, 1963, figs. 26 and 27.
70. Ibid, p.38-96.
71. Bruce-Mitford, 1974, p.242 and note 5 (p.250).
72. Akerman, 1855, pl. XV.
73. Wilson, 1971, p.135-6 and fig. 31d.
74. Musty, 1969.
75. Capelle and Vierck, 1971.
76. Laing, 1975.
77. Kendrick 1932, p.162; Kennet, D.H., Journal of the Northampton Musuem and Art Gallery, 4, 1968, pp. 5-39.
78. Wilson, 1973.
79. Henry, 1936, pl. XX, 1-4.
80. Raftery, 1966, pp. 29-38.
81. Hencken, 1935-7, pp. 191-213.
82. For the Irish group see Henry, 1956.
83. Vierck, 1970a.
84. Henry, 1936, pl. XXXII, 8.
85. Kaiseraugst: Vierck, 1970, fig.8,4: Impfingen: Vierck, 1970 a, fig.1,3.
86. See note 44.
87. Vierck, 1970.
88. Welshpool: Antiq.J., XLI, 1961, pl.x.
89. Megaw, 1963.
90. Henry, 1936, pl. XXIII, 2.
91. Fowler, 1968, p.299.
92. Stevenson, 1973.

93. Thomas, 1959; Peacock and Thomas, 1967.
94. Leeds, 1936, pl. II.
95. Haseloff, 1958.

ABBREVIATIONS

Antiq. J.	'Antiquaries Journal', London.
Arch. J.	'Archaeological Journal', London.
C.A.	'Current Archaeology', London.
D.A.B.	'Dark Age Britain', D.B. Harden, (e.d.) London, 1956.
E.C.P.M.S.	'Early Christian and Pictish Monuments of Scotland', H.M.S.O. Edinburgh, 1964.
J.R.S.	'Journal of Roman Studies', London.
J.R.S.A.I.	'Journal of the Royal Society of Antiquaries of Ireland', Dublin.
Med. Arch.	'Medieval Archaeology', London.
P.P.S.	'Proceedings of the Prehistoric Society', London.
P.R.I.A.	'Proceedings of the Royal Irish Academy', Dublin.
P.S.A.S.	'Proceedings of the Society of Antiquaries of Scotland', Edinburgh.

BIBLIOGRAPHY

Akerman, 1855 — Akerman, J.Y., *Remains of Pagan Saxondom*, London, 1855.

Alcock, 1963 — Alcock, L., *Dinas Powys*, Cardiff, 1963.

Alcock, 1971 — Alcock, L., *Arthur's Britain*, London, 1971.

Bede — *Historia Ecclesiastica Gentis Anglorum'*.

Bruce-Mitford, 1972 — Bruce-Mitford, R., Sutton Hoo, British Museum Guide, London, 1972.

Bruce-Mitford, 1974 — Bruce-Mitford, R., Aspects of Anglo-Saxon Archaeology; London, 1974.

Capelle and Vierck — Capelle, T. and Vierck, H., 'Modeln der Merowinger - und Wikingerzeit', *Frühmittelalterliche Studien*, 5, 1971.

Curie — Curle, A.O., "Report on the Excavation of a Vitrified Fort known as the Mote of Mark', *P.S.A.S.*, 48, 1913-14, pp.125-68.

Davidson and Webster — Davidson, H.R. Ellis and Webster, L. 'The Anglo-Saxon burial at Coombe (Woodnesborough), Kent', *Med. Arch.*, XI, 1967, pp.1-41.

Evison, 1963 — Evison, V.I., 'Sugar-loaf shield bosses', *Antiq.J.*, XLIII, 1963, pp. 38-96.

Evison, 1965 — Evison, V.I., *'The Fifth Century Invasions South of the Thames*, London, 1965.

Evison, 1968 — Evison, V.I., 'Quoit brooch style buckles', *Antiq.J.*, XLVIII, 1968, pp. 231-249.

Fennel — Fennel, K.R., 'Hanging-bowls with pierced escutcheons', *Med-Arch.*, IV, 1960, pp.127-8.

Foster and Daniel	Foster, I.Ll. and Daniel, G. (eds.) Prehistoric and Early Wales, London 1965.
Fowler, 1960	Fowler, E., 'The Origin and Development of the Penannular Brooch in Europe', P.P.S., XXVI, 1960.
Fowler, 1963	Fowler, E., 'Celtic Metalwork in the 5th and 6th centuries A.D.', Arch. J., CXX. 1963, pp. 98-160.
Fowler, 1968	Fowler, E., 'Hanging-Bowls', in Studies in Ancient Europe, ed. Coles and Simpson, pp. 287-310.
Fowler and Rahtz	Fowler, P. and Rahtz, P., 'Somerset, A.D. 400-700', in P.J. Fowler (ed.) Archaeology and the Landscape, pp. 187-221.
Fox	Fox, A., 'The Iron Age bowl from Rose Ash, North Devon, Antiq. J., XL1, 1961, pp. 186-198.
Frere	Frere, S.S., Britannia, London, 1975.
Gardner and Savory	Gardner, W. and Savory, H.N., Dinorben, Cardiff, 1964.
Gildas	De Excidio et Conquestu Britanniae.
Gresham	Gresham, C.A., 'The Book of Aneirin', Antiquity, XVI, 1942, pp. 237-257.
Hawkes	Hawkes, C.F.C., 'Bronze Workers, Cauldrons and Bucket Animals in Iron Age and Roman Britain', in Grimes, W.F. (ed.) Aspects of Archaeology, London, 1951, pp. 172-199.
Hawkes, 1972	Hawkes, S. Chadwick, 'A Late Roman Buckle from Tripontium', Trans. Birmingham and Warwcks. Arch. Soc., 85, 1972, pp. 145-159.

Hawkes, 1972a	Hawkes, S. Chadwick, 'More Late Roman Military Belt Fittings in Excavations at Shakenoak Farm, Part III: Site F', 1972, pp. 74-77, by A.C.C. Brodribb, A.R. Hands and D.R. Walker.
Hawkes, 1974	Hawkes, S. Chadwick, 'Some Recent Finds of Late Roman Buckles', Britannia, V, 1974, pp. 386-393.
Hawkes and Dunning	Hawkes, S.C. and Dunning, G.C., 'Soldiers and Settlers in Britain', Med. Arch., V (1961), pp. 1-70.
Haseloff	Haseloff, G., 'Fragments of a Hanging-Bowl from Bekesbourne', Med. Arch., 2, 1958, p. 72-103.
Hencken	Hencken, H. O'Neill, 'Ballinderry Crannog No. 1', P.R.I.A., XLIII, 1935-7, pp. 103-239.
Henry, 1936	Henry, F., 'Hanging-bowls', J.R.S.A.I., LXVI pt. II, 1936, pp. 209-246.
Henry, 1956	'Irish Enamels of the Dark Ages and their relation to Cloisonne techniques,' in D.A.B., pp. 71-98.
Henry, 1965	Henry, F., Irish Art in the Early Christian period to A.D. 800, London, 1965.
Kendrick, 1932	Kendrick, T.D., 'British Hanging-Bowls', Antiquity, VI, 1932, pp. 161-184.
Kendrick, 1938	Kendrick, T.D., Anglo-Saxon Art to A.D. 900, London, 1938.
Kilbride-Jones, 1935-6	Kilbride-Jones, H.E., 'Scots Zoomorphic Penannular Brooches', P.S.A.S., LXX, 1935-6, pp. 124-38.
Kilbride-Jones, 1936-7	Kilbride-Jones, H.E., 'A Bronze Hanging-Bowl from Castle Tioram, Moidart: and a suggested absolute Chronology for British Hanging-Bowls', P.S.A.S., LXXI, 1936-7, pp. 206-247.

Kilbride-Jones, 1937-8	Kilbride-Jones, H.E., 'The Evolution of Penannular Brooches with Zoomorphic Terminals in Great Britain and Ireland', P.R.I.A. XLIII, 1935-7, pp. 379-455.
Laing, 1973	Laing, L.R., 'The Mote of Mark', C.A., 39, July 1973, pp. 121-5.
Laing, 1975	Laing, L.R., 'The Mote of Mark and the Origins of Celtic Interlace', Antiquity, XLIX, 1975, pp. 98-108.
Leeds, 1936	Leeds, E.T., Early Anglo-Saxon Art and Archaeology, Oxford, 1936.
Leeds, 1945	Leeds, E.T., 'The distribution of the Angles and Saxons Archaeologically considered', Archaeologia, 91, 1945, pp. 1-106.
Megaw	Megaw, J.V.S., 'A British bronze bowl of the Belgic Iron Age from Poland', Antiq.J., XLIII, 1963, pp. 27-37.
Musty	Musty, J., 'The Excavation of Two Barrows, one of Saxon date, at Ford, Laverstock, near Salisbury, Wilts.', Antiq.J., XLIX, 1969, pp. 98-117.
Myres, 1956	Myres, J.N.L., 'Romano-Saxon Pottery', in D.A.B., pp. 16-39.
Myres, 1969	Myres, J.N.L., Anglo-Saxon Pottery and the Settlement of England, Oxford, 1969.
Ozanne	Ozanne, A., 'The Peak Dwellers', Med. Arch., 6-7, 1962-3, pp. 15-52.
Peacock and Thomas	Peacock, D. and Thomas, A.C., 'Class E imported Post-Roman Pottery: A suggested origin' Cornish Archaeology, 6, 1967, pp. 35-46.
Peers and Radford	Peers, C. and Radford, C.A.R., 'The Saxon Monastery of Whitby', Archaeologia, 89, 1943.

Raftery	Raftery, J., 'The Cuillard and other Unpublished Hanging-Bowls', J.R.S.A.I., vol. 96 pt. 1, 1966, pp. 29-38.
Savory, 1956	Savory, H.N., 'Some sub-Romano-British brooches from South Wales', in D.A.B., pp. 40-58.
Stevenson, 1973	Stevenson, R.B.K., 'The Hanging-Bowl Mould', in A. Small and M.B. Cottam, Craig Phadrig, Univ. of Dundee Dept. of Geog. Occ. Papers, 1973, No. 1, pp. 49-51.
Thomas, 1959	Thomas, A.C., 'Imported Pottery in Dark Age Western Britain', Med. Arch., 3, 1959, pp. 89-111.
Thomas, 1961	Thomas, A.C., 'Animal Art of the Scottish Iron Age', Arch.J., 118, 1961, pp. 14-63.
Thomas, 1971	Thomas, A.C., Britain and Ireland in Early Christian Times, London, 1971.
Vierck, 1970	Vierck, H., 'Cortina Tripodis: zu Aufhängung und Gebrauch Subrömischer Hangebecken aus Britannien und Irland', Frühmittelalterliche Studien, 4, 1970, pp. 8-52.
Vierck, 1970a	Vierck, H., 'Cortina Tripodis: ein Beispiel spätantiker Traditionen der Insularen Mission; Praehistorische Zeitschrift, 45, 1970, pp. 236-240.
Wainwright, 1955	Wainwright, F.T. (ed.) The Problem of the Picts, Edinburgh and London, 1955.
Wedlake, 1958	Wedlake, W.J., Excavations at Camerton, Camerton Excavation Club, 1958.
Wheeler, 1932	Wheeler, R.E.M., 'The Paradox of Celtic Art', Antiquity, VI (1932) pp. 292-300.
Wheeler, 1932a	Wheeler, R.E.M., Report on the Excavation of the Prehistoric, Roman and Post Roman Site in Lydney Park, Glos, London, 1932.

Wilson, 1971   Wilson, D.M., <u>The Anglo-Saxons</u>, Harmondsworth, 1971.

Wilson, 1973   Wilson, D.M., 'The Metalwork', in <u>St. Ninian's Isle and its Treasure</u>, University of Aberdeen, 1973, vol. I text, vol. II plates.

www.ingramcontent.com/pod-product-compliance
Ingram Content Group UK Ltd.
Pitfield, Milton Keynes, MK11 3LW, UK
UKHW061214180426
11947UKWH00029B/2041